CALLED
—⚬⚭ TO ⚭⚬—
WORK

E. JAMES DUBOIS

ISBN 978-1-63874-783-3 (paperback)
ISBN 978-1-63874-784-0 (digital)

Christian Faith Publishing, Inc.
832 Park Avenue
Meadville, PA 16335
www.christianfaithpublishing.com

Printed in the United States of America

As they ministered to the Lord and fasted, the
Holy Spirit said, Separate me Barnabas and Saul
for the work unto which I have called them.

—Acts 13:2

In dedication to those who were "called to work:"

- Christina DuBois-my helpmate in life and ministry
- Rev. Charles* H. DuBois-my grand pop
- Rev. Edward* Walter Cooper-pastor
- Dr., Rev. Evan* Pedrick-chaplain and friend
- Rev. Benjamin* and Caroline* Taylor-pastor
- Dr., Rev. Norman* W. Paullin-neighbor and friend
- Dr., Rev. Edwin* and Agnes* Bustard-neighbors
- Rev. Paul* and Jane Pedrick-coworker and friends
- Rev. Dale and Karen Bossley-friends
- Rev. John* and Mary Shipley-friends
- Rev. Lee and Judy Harrison-friends
- Rev. Jerry and Carol Smith-coworker and friends
- Rev. Charles and Jane Serbeck-coworker and friends
- Mark and Lisa Gebhardt-pastor
- Manny* and Eleanor* Knaus-missionaries
- Rev. Don* Reynolds-missionary and co worker
- William Cawman-coworker
- Carol Malone-coworker
- Rev. Randy and Julie Jackson-pastor

*deceased

CONTRIBUTORS

- Dale Bossley
- William Cawman
- Dorothy M. DuBois (1930–1981)
- Jacob E. DuBois
- Joshua T. DuBois
- Gail Haslett
- Heidi Koering
- Carol Malone
- Susan Muller
- Jane Pedrick
- Charles Serbeck
- Mary Shipley
- Jerry Smith

CHAPTER 1

WHY THIS BOOK?

I am currently in my retirement years after forty-two years of ministry. While playing in my garden, I began to reflect on my previous ministry opportunities. Like Barnabas and Saul, I experienced what I believe to be a call for the work which was then set before me. I believe the reality of being called to a work has been an interesting process. As such, my purpose in writing this book is to highlight some practical experiences to help discern or better understand the possible calling of God to a specific vocational ministry.

Wait…don't hang up yet. The calling of God to a specific work may or may not be that of being a minister, teacher, missionary, or college professor. Any of which would be a noble calling. However, don't minimize the calling of God to a specific work such as a table waiter (deacon) or a prison volunteer, parent, friend, business owner, soldier, or musician. A response in obedience to any work assigned by God can be life changing for you and to those who benefited by your ministry.

Boyce's side of the conversation. As such, we could only presume to know what Saint Peter was supposedly speaking by the things Dr. Boice was saying.

The use of a telephone in this eulogy was an effective way of communicating the earthly accomplishments of the deceased. In addition, it was also an effective way of communicating the only means of salvation by grace through faith.

For by grace are ye saved through faith; and that not of yourselves, it is the gift of God, not of works, lest any man should boast. For we are his workmanship, created in Christ Jesus unto good works, which God hath before ordained that we should walk in them. (Ephesians 2:8–10)

The idea of God calling us via a telephone could be considered gauche or just plain immature. However, the Bible does expound on the various ways in which God communicates to us through His Word.

God, who at sundry times and in diverse manners spoke in times past unto the fathers by the prophets, hath in these last days spoken unto us by His Son, whom he hath appointed heir of all things, by whom also he made the worlds; Who, being the brightness of his glory, and the express image of his person, and upholding all things by the word of his power, when he had by himself purged our sins, sat down on the right hand of the Majesty on high. (Hebrews 1:1–3)

I am not suggesting that we should actually expect to receive a telephone call from God. However, like our phone, you could receive an unexpected call to work through His Word. Therefore, throughout this book, I will include the simple image of an old dial telephone along with key passages of Scripture. Consider the possibility that God may be calling through that particular portion of Scripture.

CHAPTER 3

THE UNEXPECTED CALL

As a member of the boomer age group, I was blessed to live life to the fullest in the renowned '60s. Yes, my wife had a flower painted on her car, and I was often known for street racing in my '55 Chevy. I was also known not to be an exceptional student. The last place I would be expected to be is standing up as a speaker in front of a large group. I failed a history class in my junior year of high school because I refused to give an assigned oral report. My complete lack of confidence was only one factor in my refusal. The teacher had little to no control of the class. Therefore, the students were rude and obnoxious towards those giving their oral reports. I just flat out refused to comply with the assignment and taught that teacher a lesson. Well actually, I had to make up the class in summer school.

I was also of the age group subject to the military draft. As such, I did serve in the US Army as an air traffic controller. My wife has said my experiences in Vietnam did change me. Like many other veterans, I have found it hard to discuss some war experiences. I did attempt to address some of these experiences through my writing of a novel entitled *The Pathfinder*.

Life after Vietnam was a challenge. Finding a job at that time was even more challenging. Raising a family in those days was interesting. After years of bouncing from job to job, a longtime friend of the family finally hired me. The late Fred Borhen was highly respected and a craftsman custom homebuilder. I had finally landed my dream job.

During those post-war years, my wife and I began to get involved in our local church. We took on a church volunteer job as youth leaders. It was fun! Youth leadership was exciting and rewarding in many unexpected ways.

We were fortunate to be able to plan a big event for our church youth group. We were excited about taking our youth group to a big conference at the Thomas Road Baptist Church in Lynchburg, Virginia. These were the years when the late Rev. Jerry Falwell was planning to establish a Christian college. That college is now the nationally respected Liberty University. It was exciting to have our youth group interact with other teens and gifted speakers and interact in stimulating activities at this youth conference.

During this conference, we were pleased to participate in a major worship service. I recall the excitement of probably five thousand youth and the beautiful music created by these young voices. The speaker gave a challenging message on David and Goliath. At the end of the message, the speaker issued an invitational challenge. Who among this huge group of young people would respond to a calling to full-time Christian service? At that time in my life, I had probably heard a pastor or teacher expound on the biblical account of David and Goliath a dozen times. However, this time, I felt like everything said was being aimed directly to me. When the invitation was given, I took my wife by her hand, and we had a brief discussion regarding the invitation, and together, we went forward in response to this calling. As we knelt at the altar, I took notice that only two couples had responded to the calling. Not one young person responded. Only four people, two married couples, responded.

Okay, what does it mean to respond to a calling to full-time Christian service? When my wife and I returned home from the youth conference, I was anxious to tell my mother and other family members. While my mother was supportive, some others were less than reassuring. I believe some of the naysayers were basing their response upon a correct assessment of my lack of abilities. At the time of my calling, I did not demonstrate any of the essential qualities of a pastor. Why would God call me?

When I told my neighbor, Dr. Edwin Bustard, that we had dedicated our lives to full-time Christian service, he said, "You need to go to Bible College." He recommended that I attend Philadelphia College of Bible.

Now this calling was beginning to get complicated. How could I go to college when I had a full-time job? Remember my dream job? I needed to work through this problem on my terms. I thought I knew how to resolve this dilemma. I would keep my job and go to college at night school. You know how this works. I get to do what I want, and at the same time, I am doing what is expected of me. Perfect. I then applied for enrollment at Philadelphia College of Bible. It was late in the summer when I had applied, and I didn't think my application would even be considered for the new school year.

On a Thursday night, I received a telephone call from a representative for Philadelphia College of Bible. Surprisingly, I was accepted as a student and was told to report as a new student on the following Monday morning.

I asked, "Why am I expected to report for classes on a Monday morning? I have a job. Since I applied for night classes, I should be expected to attend classes on Monday night."

The college representative said, "Sir, your application was for day classes, and you should report on Monday morning."

My plan didn't work. Therefore, I learned my first lesson in responding to a divine calling. Don't try to do things your way.

For my thoughts are not your thoughts, neither are your ways my ways, saith the LORD. (Isaiah 55:8)

As I went to work on the Friday following my acceptance as a full-time student to Bible College, I somehow needed to tell Mr. Borhen that I had to quit. And I couldn't give him a two-week notice. In fact, that would be my last day at work. According to the normal practice on the job site, we started work early and stopped for lunch at noon. Mrs. Elsie Borhen always brought lunch for her husband. We all sat at a picnic table for lunch. Lunch break was when I was going to drop the bomb. I explained the need for my reporting to college on Monday morning. I will never forget how Mr. Borhen responded to my announcement that I was going to quit.

He said, "Jim, I have learned to never get in the way of the Lord." Then he turned to his wife and said, "Elsie, you give Jim two weeks of extra pay."

Wait. I didn't give a two-week notice, and yet I walked away with two weeks of extra pay. Mr. Borhen taught me a lot about building custom homes. However, Mr. Borhen also taught me much more about a Christian's response to God. That is, never get in the way of the Lord.

When I look back at my calling, I have seen how God used His Word, His people, and circumstances under His control to confirm a calling to full-time Christian service. This was just the start. What a journey and a blessing.

So as a college student without a job, how could I pay the bills and put food on the table? Well, I applied for my veteran's educational benefits, and my wife took a job. I hope the reality of responding to a divine call to work also demonstrates that we have a responsibility to make our calling and election sure (2 Peter 1:11).

CHAPTER 4

CALLED *TO* A CHURCH

Following my graduation from the Philadelphia College of Bible, I was recognized by my local church and set on a path for ordination as a pastor. It was an honor to be examined by a council of local pastors and formally ordained by the church of my youth. This ordination set into motion my first journey in seeking a pastoral ministry.

The process of seeking a pastoral ministry should result in a mutual acknowledgement that the local body of Christ desires a specific candidate and that same candidate feels called to shepherd that particular flock. I participated in this process within every imaginable scenario. In some cases, the church did not want me, and in other cases, I did not want to work with them. I remember one particular church which was in such a state of disarray that I said to my wife, "If God wants me in that church, He is going to need to physically plant me in that church." Thankfully, that assignment was not in God's plan.

I received an invitation to preach at a church in the northern Boston area of Massachusetts. The initial invite was just an opportunity for the church to see if they actually wanted to extend a formal invitation for me to be considered as a candidate. The church building was beautiful. The congregation was warm and welcoming. The size of the church was much larger than any of my expectations. The entire initial meeting was exciting. As my wife and I were returning home, we agreed that the initial experience was great but they would never extend a call to me.

To my surprise, the church in Massachusetts did extend an invitation for me to be considered as a candidate. Now, the process of a divine calling becomes a little more complex. The church needs to be assured they are calling the right pastor. At the same time, the pastor needs to be assured he is in the place God wants him to serve.

The process of my candidacy included a response to documents requested by the church. I answered their questions, submitted a complete statement of faith, and tendered the required letters of reference. I requested a letter of reference from my pastor, one from a college professor, and my neighbor Dr. Bustard. Unfortunately for me, Dr. Bustard had his glorious homecoming prior to submitting my letter of reference. Dr. Bustard's passing opened the door for Mrs. Bustard to submit the letter of reference on behalf of her husband. This little twist in the process was a little unnerving. I had a pretty good sense of how Dr. Bustard would respond. I wasn't so sure of how Mrs. Bustard would respond. Mrs. Bustard had a reputation of being strong willed, outspoken, and a real student of the Bible. Later, in my meeting with the church officials, the letter of reference from Mrs. Bustard was raised. Apparently, the letter was an entirely biblical response. I was never shown the letter. However, it was described as a two-column multiple page document. On the left column was a listing of all the biblical qualifications for an elder as outlined in 1 Timothy 3:1-7. On the right column, Mrs. Bustard made her comments with respect to my level of satisfying each and every biblical qualification for an elder.

It appears that the calling by God to work according to His good pleasure involves a reasonable level of education, recognition of God's leading in your life, and a process of examination.

These things command and teach. Let no man despise thy youth, but be thou an example of the believers, in word, in conduct, in love, in spirit, in faith, in purity. (1 Timothy 4:11–12)

CALVARY BAPTIST CHURCH

The church in the Boston area did, in fact, extend a calling for me to serve as their pastor. My purpose in writing this book is not to list the accomplishments or failures in this or other ministries. However, I do want to remain focused on the concept of a call by God to work. Having said this, I wish to share the calling by God to work within the framework of ministries. The church of my youth saw the calling by God of three pastors, with myself being one of the three.

While serving as the pastor to the church in the Boston area, our ministry saw the calling by God for a young lady to be a missionary to France. The commissioning of this missionary marked a significant milestone. The local church was experiencing a personal expansion of its ministry to the mission field. We can all appreciate the local church's support to missions. However, having one of your own being called by God to the mission field makes the financial support, prayer support, and interest in the ministry all that much more personal.

In addition, our church was associated with a small independent denomination which had a deep interest in missionary outreach to the Russian and Ukrainian peoples. To better support its outreach, the denomination was planning to construct a missionary complex. This endeavor was designed to include housing, conference rooms, printing presses, and two sound recording studios. Our church was committed to support this project with finances and with hands-on construction. As such, we planned several workdays, and volunteers would go to the construction site and do whatever they were capable of doing.

Given my experience in home construction, I was looking forward to volunteering at the missionary complex. I was looking forward to swinging a hammer. My initial evaluation of the construction site was exciting. The entire complex was being supervised by a missionary organization which did construction projects for missionaries. Wow! What a group! This group would build homes, conference centers, camps, schools, and other things necessary for missionaries. The group would use its relationship with large suppliers and seek donations of materials for a construction project. They would reach out to Christian contractors and seek donations or reduced costs for equipment or services.

Each workday, the entire work crew was invited to a morning coffee break with home-baked goodies and a Bible study. On any given day, some of the work crew was representative of the local municipal electric company, phone companies, contractors, inspectors, or even delivery persons. All were invited to the coffee break and heard a clear presentation of the Gospel.

During my first visit as a volunteer to the construction site, I was introduced to Manny and Eleanor Knaus. This couple was well advanced in age. They were missionaries and members of the team responsible for the construction of the complex. Manny was specifically responsible for the woodwork, cabinet building, and trim work. Manny was a craftsman. Eleanor was specifically responsible for the baked goods for the morning coffee breaks. I was impressed with this couple for many reasons. However, to stay focused on the calling to work, I recall Manny and Eleanor related to me how they were retired and enjoying the golden years of life when they felt a calling by God to use their skills in missions. They were introduced to the missionary construction team and responded even in retirement. They sold their home, bought a camper trailer, raised support as missionaries, and began to work. Manny and Eleanor were beginning to show some effects of aging with some loss of strength and agility, but their hearts and dedication to use their skills was a tribute to their calling. Wow! A retired craftsman and wife were called by God to use their skills in a ministry to missionaries.

CHAPTER 5

CALLED *FROM* A CHURCH

The calling of God to work may result in a lifelong assignment to one specific ministry. That may happen. However, it's probably more likely that God may occasionally move someone to a new assignment. I found it interesting how God called me *from* my first church to a new assignment.

My first church ministry was going through a transition. We had a funeral and the birth of a new baby every month for twelve months straight. However, as mentioned earlier, I wish to stay focused on the issues of a calling. As we were approaching the Thanksgiving and Christmas season, I had no specific thoughts of leaving this ministry. During a particular officers' meeting, I had a very unusual experience. The officers meeting was progressing in a rather routine manner, yet I felt detached from the meeting. Sort of like I was observing rather than participating. After the meeting was over and everyone went home, I began reflecting on what had just happened. It seemed like I was being excluded from the future planning of this ministry. Was God telling me it was time to move on?

When I arrived at home, I told my wife of my experience at the officers' meeting. That night, I received a telephone call from a friend from Virginia. It was probably around 11:30 p.m. when my friend called. Given the late hour, I immediately thought something was wrong. My friend, Ronnie Snell, said, "I called to tell you our church is looking for a pastor."

I said, "You called me at 11:30 p.m. to tell me your church is looking for a pastor?"

Ronnie said, "Yeah, I just had to call you. I was in bed but I couldn't sleep."

I asked, "How long has your church been looking for a pastor?"

Ronnie said, "For about three months."

I asked, "Why did you feel the need to call me tonight?"

Ronnie said, "I don't know. I went to bed and just couldn't go to sleep. I had to get up and call you."

I shared with Ronnie what had happened earlier that evening at the officers' meeting. I told Ronnie that his telephone call might have been a confirmation that it was time to leave this ministry. It was. I felt at complete peace that it was time to leave this ministry. However, I had no place to go. I was leaving with no new assignment. Was this the end? No new ministry.

I needed to provide for my family, so I called my father and asked him to locate a home for us to move into by January 1. My father came through and found a home for us. We began packing and ultimately rented a large box truck for the move back to our hometown. Moving day was the last day in December. Our prayers for God to open a new ministry seemed to go unheard.

The burden which Habakkuk the prophet, did see. O LORD, how long shall I cry out unto Thee of violence, and Thou wilt not save! Behold

among the nations, with regard, and wonder marvelously; for I will work a work in your days, which you will not believe, though it be told to you. (Habakkuk 1:1–2, 5)

As we were unloading the moving truck, my father came over and said, "I got a call from Bob Josephson. He wants to know if you will preach at their church tomorrow."

In my frustration and with a bad attitude, I said, "No. I can't preach tomorrow. Tell them I will preach next week."

I had thereby committed to preach as a pulpit supply at a new church on the next Sunday. During the week leading up to that commitment, my mother passed away. I did preach at Bob Josephson's church as planned. That particular preaching experience ultimately led to a thirteen-year pastoral assignment.

It was an amazing experience to realize that God had not only called me to a work, but in fact, He did work a work that would be regarded and wondered at marvelously.

This new pastoral assignment was quite different from that of my first church experience. The new assignment was a small church which required that I find a job to support my family. As a glimpse into a contrast, the first church I served in was a wealthy congregation with all the best that money could buy. This new church assignment provided a weekly salary of $25. My wife and I laughed because three weekly trips to church for Sunday morning and Sunday night and Wednesday night services required an amount of gasoline which exceeded the weekly salary. We also laughed at the fact that Wednesday night prayer meetings involved two people praying among those in attendance. My wife would pray, and I would close in prayer, and then we would go home.

At first, I thought the calling from the big church to the small church was a demotion of some sort. It wasn't. New and greater opportunities opened. Ultimately, the work that God did in this little church was incredible. The congregation grew in numbers and spiritually. The building complex and property were more than doubled in size. And again, staying with the purpose of our topic of a calling to work, a member of our church was called by God into a pastoral ministry. John Shipley was a union electrician, and he had a disdain for pastors. Yes, John Shipley had a low opinion of the clergy and did not hide his opinions. However, God did a work in John's life which was indeed amazing. John Shipley was called by God to work as a pastor.

John Shipley died at the apex of raising a young family. The following is how John's wife, Mary, describes their calling to ministry:

> John felt God's call into ministry as a teenager. He specifically felt that God was calling him into ministry with children through Child Evangelism Fellowship. When he expressed this to his parents, his father—who was not a believer at the time—forbade him. As a result, John followed his father, brother, uncle, and grandfather into the "family business," which was to become a union electrician. When we married in 1973, John was a second-year apprentice. He was assured of a decent living with a good trade.
>
> After we were married for twelve years with two children, John again felt God's call into full-time service. When our pastor, Jim DuBois, announced one Sunday that Philadelphia College of Bible was offering courses at satellite locations, John felt that this was meant for him. He continued to work full time as an electrician and took Bible courses in the evening. On day John told me that part time was not enough and that he needed to attend full time. Since we were living in our first house, this was no small decision. It meant selling our home, moving in with my widowed mother-in-law, and transferring our children to a different school. I was finally finishing my music education degree after many years of hard work and was looking forward to using it.

But God's timing is perfect, and He was preparing me for this change. The house that I loved developed issues that detached me from it. We were influenced by the example of our pastor and his wife, Jim and Chris DuBois, who demonstrated the joy of serving God together as a team. When John asked, I was ready to agree.

Our lives underwent some drastic changes. Financially, we lost John's income for almost four years. I accepted a position teaching junior high subjects in the Christian school our children attended. After John finished his degree, he served as interim pastor twice, as an assistant pastor and, ultimately, as pastor of a small church. After John became ill with cancer, he continued to teach adult Sunday school and served as pulpit supply for area churches. When John went home to be with the Lord in 2010, he was only fifty-eight but felt that he had completed the ministry that God had laid out for him.

Looking back, I realize that if we had not answered God's call, we would have missed out on numerous exciting experiences and challenges. God stretched both of us as we experienced His grace and provision countless times. We came to realize that God used us in ministries that He had uniquely prepared and gifted us for. I am thankful for the years of service that we experienced together and continue to look for opportunities to serve the Lord.

One of the major blessings in serving as a pastor is seeing how God works in the lives of some parishioners. My wife and I enjoyed seeing John and Mary grow spiritually. John took on some challenging ministries and developed into a solid biblical preacher. Even in illness, John had a unique sense of humor. John used humor to disarm and insert spiritual truths as a witness to an unexpected nurse, doctor, or hospital volunteer.

I also had to learn another lesson in being called *from* a ministry **to** another. Around my two-and-a-half year mark at my second church, I was teaching at a Christian school as my primary means of providing for my family. I loved the teaching job and began feeling that this alone would be my full-time ministry. I gave the church officers my notice of resignation with a timeline of six months. They had until the end of December to find another pastor. As the weeks progressed, the officers didn't seem to be motivated to find another pastor. I was getting frustrated with their lack of effort in finding a replacement. So be it, I thought. That's their problem.

I fulfilled my obligation to the six-month time frame. I preached my final sermon on the last Sunday of December. At the conclusion of the service, a widow with her three young daughters approached me and asked if I would assist her in having her daughters dedicated to the Lord. We had come to know this mother and her daughters in the previous months. She had started to attend church on a regular basis following the death of her husband. In fact, her first appearance at our church was with an introduction. She said, "Hello, my name is J, and I just buried my husband." I have no idea why J waited until after my final sermon on the last day of December to ask for a dedication service. I certainly was not going to turn down an opportunity to dedicate these young girls to the Lord. The following Sunday was available because the officers didn't bother to find anyone to preach.

I preached my final *final* sermon at this church on the first Sunday in January, which included a dedication service as requested by the widow. Immediately following the Sunday service, as most of the congregation was proceeding to exit to the rear of the sanctuary, a member of the church approached the pulpit in a rather loud manner, and wagging her finger, she said, "I still think you are supposed to be our pastor." I believe it was two days later that this young mother was killed in a terrible automobile accident. Her car was T-boned by a commercial plumbing truck. I was called upon to identify the body. I was also called upon to conduct the funeral service.

On the third Sunday of January, I was asked to preach again. I had to consider the words of being called to pastor this small church. I gave a blistering sermon on a lack of commitment, which was clearly and correctly aimed at myself. I addressed my failures, and with God's blessing, I remained at this church for another ten years. It was another lesson learned. Don't try to leave a ministry until the phone rings!

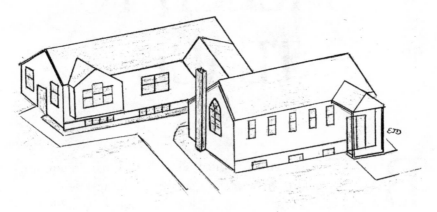

Estell Manor Community Church

CHAPTER 6

CALLED TO TEACH

Being called to a small country church may require employment to care for the needs of the family. The apostle Paul was described as a tent maker, which allowed him to avoid being a burden to the local churches.

In my search for employment, I felt led to apply for a teaching position at Cumberland Christian School (CCS). I was intimately familiar with this school in that I was a former student. In addition, our children were students in this school.

The experience of teaching in a K-12 setting was rewarding in many ways. At that time, the school was adding the high-school grades, and I was called on to help establish the middle-school concept under the skillful leadership of Jerry Smith. Mr. Smith was the headmaster for a number of years and wisely guided a responsible expansion of the school. This meant new class activities, development of new curricula, and the teaching of new subjects. During this period of time, I was also able to continue with my own graduate studies. I attended the Eastern Mennonite College in Harrisonburg,

Virginia, during summer sessions. I eventually completed my master's degree with the California Graduate School of Theology, Glendale, California.

In keeping with the theme of this book, I want to give a peek into the future from the standpoint of the possibility of God calling some of these students to work. For now, I want to just mention some names. Later in this book, I will expand upon a couple of these students.

- Tracy Hill-future missionary
- Greg H-future pastor
- Heidi Koering-future CCS school board president
- Dorothy Pacitto-future CCS school board member
- Mark Gebhardt-future CCS teacher, guidance counselor, and pastor

These are some students that I had direct contact with during the three years of ministry at Cumberland Christian School. Can you imagine the overall impact of this school upon students given its now seventy-five years of ministry? Praise the Lord!

The growth, development, and expansion of Cumberland Christian School has, and continues to be, a result of God's blessings and His calling of leaders, teachers, and supporting churches for a number of years. I identified Jerry Smith as one of the persons called by God to lead in the greater expansion of the school. The following is Jerry Smith's recollection of his calling to a teaching ministry:

> As for my "calling," it is difficult to put into words. I felt called the moment I accepted Christ when I was thirteen years old. I had no idea of what I would do in the future, but I felt that my life was a calling to serve Him. I hope that doesn't seem hyper-spiritual, but as I look back, I have simply tried to serve God in whatever circumstances I was. It might be while working in Sears as a salesman or working in construction or

as a student—I was called to serve God in every endeavor. I did my best and tried to be a witness for Him. Did I always do an excellent job? No. But while I failed at many points, I can say that the general has usually been to serve His calling in my life.

As for His guidance, I pretty much took one step at a time in my daily living and at certain junctures; the Lord gave me strong impressions. They were not always clear, yet they were clear enough to tell me at the time. I tried to empty myself of all my own desires and allow Him to speak to me. Frankly, I have been amazed at how that has happened so many times.

I will give you one example: I was pastoring a small church in Pocahontas, Illinois. Pocahontas was a town of less than six hundred people. It was the hog-raising capital of southern Illinois, and it was the only "wet" town in a "dry" county. Those were the two areas the town claimed for fame. As a pastor, many parishioners raised hogs. If the sow were giving birth, the farmer would stay with the sow continually to help the delivery because each piglet was valuable. If the farmer was away for some reason, I quickly learned that the pastor was expected to help out and take his place. I only pastored this church for about nine months, but I learned an awful lot of valuable insight into ministry during those months.

But I had only been there five months when I felt the Lord was leading me to resign. Things were not going badly. We finished a small building addition, and I was starting to develop as a teacher-preacher, but there was a nagging feeling in my spirit. Was I failing? Was I discouraged? What would the people say if I resigned after such a short time? They would be discouraged, and I would appear to have called it "quits" too early. The nagging feeling did not go away. I spoke with my wife Carol about it. I prayed. And I got an "impression" that I should resign as of the second week of January. That was so specific that it seemed questionable. But I could not shake it after meditating on it for two months.

So in November, I informed the board that I intended to resign effective the second week of January. I continued to minister as hard as before, but I also began to send out resumes in every direction and for every type ministry I could envision. There was no return interest. Nothing. Nada. After the first week of January, I met with the church board; they asked what I was going to do. I didn't have an answer. I responded by saying that while I didn't know, I still planned to preach the coming Sunday and trust God to lead me after that.

But on that Friday, I received a call from a Christian school in Ohio. Their first-grade teacher had to resign unexpectedly, and they needed someone now. I preached a sermon on Sunday. On Monday, I traveled to Ohio to interview. By that Friday, my family (wife, son, and our few possessions) were moved to Ohio, and I started teaching the following Monday. The following year, I was appointed to become the principal of that school.

I cannot explain, but something similar has happened for every job I have had—at Cumberland Christian School, teaching at Cumberland County College, or pastoring at Greentree Church.

The year I left Cumberland Christian School was not a surprise to me. I had an impression five years earlier that I would be leaving that year (which was my thirtieth year).

I find it interesting that Jerry Smith was involved in a pastorate and was led into long-term teaching and administrative positions of leadership in Christian schools. My experience was about to take on another unexpected twist. I now confess to the reader I spent the next twenty-three years in state prisons.

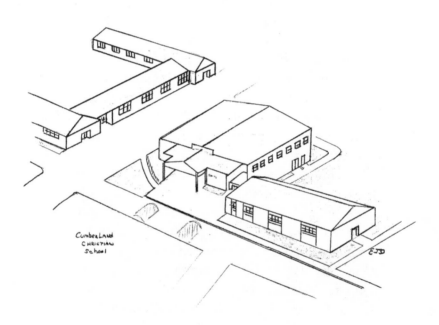

CumberLand
CHRISTIAN
School

Chapter 7

CALLED TO PRISON

Actually, God called me to a ministry that I had not expected in any way, shape, or form. During my college years, I was required to do Christian service volunteer work in various ministries. At that time, Rev. Paul Pedrick, supervisor of chaplaincy services at Bayside State Prison, Leesburg, New Jersey, invited me to volunteer for a year at the prison. I found the prison ministry interesting, challenging, and rewarding. The late Chaplain Pedrick was a personal friend and someone I considered to be a spiritual giant. He was also a masterful musician. Paul played the saxophone for the US Navy band. However, he was better known for playing the piano. One character trait of Paul, known by some, was his ability to pull off a joke once in a while. I know because I was often the butt of one of his jokes.

On one particular occasion, Chaplain Pedrick called me to the prison for a chat. The invitation for a chat was not a joke. Actually, the meeting resulted in a job offer for me to serve as a prison chaplain. Chaplain Pedrick reflected on the success of my volunteer services and said he felt led to offer me the position. The uniqueness of the chaplaincy allowed for me to continue the ministry at the small church while working as a chaplain. The worship services at the prison were easily scheduled at early or late times. This arrangement resulted in a busy schedule on Sundays. Preaching once on Sunday at the prison and twice at the church on the same day set in motion the weekly nap on Sunday afternoons.

Why would God call me to a prison ministry? I was comfortable working in a prison setting, yet it was nothing I ever dreamed of doing. Was this new assignment another demotion? I went from a large church to a small church. I then went from an active Christian school working with teens to a state prison working with hardened criminals. Remember the passage in Habakkuk referenced earlier in this book (chapter 5) where God says He is doing a work that we should marvel upon? Think of this, God was calling me to work while He is doing His work in me. Wow! I was not only called to work as a chaplain, but ultimately, I would later be given the opportunity to supervise all of the chaplains within the New Jersey Department of Corrections and Department of Mental Health Services. Yes, that means I ultimately became the boss over Chaplain Pedrick. See, the ultimate joke was on him every time he called me "boss." My ministry went from one school to twelve state prisons, three state mental health facilities, and twenty county jails. I went from being a volunteer to overseeing an army of volunteers.

Now let's explore the possibility of God calling individuals to work *from* prison. Well, I will give you only two examples. One is an example of a prisoner. The second example is a prison correctional officer (please don't call them "guards").

During one prison assignment, I hired an inmate to be my clerk. Yes, inmates could work and get paid. The money paid to prisoners was minimal, but it could help buy things from the commissary. God called this particular inmate to salvation. Over a long period of time, the inmate began studying and later actually leading Bible studies with fellow inmates. He did a lot of self-study, but on many occasions, he would come to me and ask, "Chaplain DuBois, what is your opinion of this passage of Scripture?"

My standard reply was, "You don't want my opinion on anything because opinions change. What does the Bible say? Let the Bible stand as your one and only guide."

This particular inmate ultimately felt the calling of God to be a minister. Upon his release from prison, I directed him to a biblical church that assisted him in his studies and, ultimately, into the pastorate. Sadly, upon the day of this inmate's release, his son was being processed into state prison. The cycle of incarceration remains to be a tragic reality.

In another setting, I had senior correctional officer Charles Serbeck come to my office with questions, questions, and questions. I came to believe some of the questions were designed as intentionally provocative. In fact, I wasn't sure if the officer was genuinely seeking answers or if he just enjoyed provoking. Ultimately, over a long period of time, this officer was called by God to work. In retirement, he satisfied all the requirements for his church in education and ordination and now serves as pastor for visitation in his local church.

The following is how Chuck Serbeck describes his calling:

> The call on my life comes from the book of Acts, chapter six (Stephen's ministry). Listening to this call has blessed me in many different ways. It has prepared me to minister to many during my time in New Jersey and New York City during 9/11 as well as during and after the murder of one of my fellow officers.
>
> Now God is using me in ministering to seniors who are hospitalized and homebound in ways that I could have never imagined. Even through volunteering as a chaplain in local hospitals, God has placed many new people in my life. The ironic thing for me in this is even though God has allowed many different venues, I have been blessed in ways that are indescribable.

CHAPTER 8

CALLED TO A CHALLENGE

D uring a time of prison expansion in New Jersey, plans were being developed for the construction of its largest state prison. The new South Woods State Prison was being built to accommodate three thousand three hundred inmates along with a hospital and a massive state industrial complex. The design of the prison allowed for the entire prison to be divided into three completely independent facilities. Thus, each unit would accommodate a population of one thousand inmates. Additional areas included a hospital and minimum custody facility and a completely separate administrative complex. Due to the demand for bed space, each of the three facilities was filled as each unit was built.

I received a call from the newly appointed administrator of South Woods State Prison asking me to serve as the supervisor of chaplaincy services. This promotion was an exciting opportunity to develop a completely new chaplaincy program with new staff, new volunteer groups, and the development of policy and procedures for the chaplaincy department.

This new assignment also gave me a different perspective on the topic of God's calling to work. Now, for the first time, I was in a position to hire new employees and to bring into the prison facility new volunteer groups. I was in a position to interview chaplains from all different faith groups. It was interesting to hear how a catholic priest, or rabbi, fellow pastors, or an imam describe his calling to a ministry. It was also interesting to hear how volunteers rely on God's calling to do His good work. It was equally interesting to hear how many people have absolutely no concept of a calling. Sadly, for some religious leaders, their involvement in ministry is nothing more than a career choice.

In the midst of establishing the chaplaincy program at South Woods State Prison, there were some discussions of the retirement of the state coordinator of chaplaincy services. This position was responsible for the oversight of all the chaplaincy services for the New Jersey Departments of Corrections and the Department of Mental Health Services. This was a significant upper level management position based in Trenton. I was asked to submit a letter of interest in this position. It was an honor to be considered. However, I really didn't want to take the position. I did write a letter, but it was carefully written to imply my services would better be utilized in the building of the new services at the South Woods State Prison. I was hoping to be politically sensitive to those in power while saying thank you but no thanks.

(Author's note: I have been unable to contact and obtain permission to use the actual name with the individual hereafter referred to as director Robert S.)

It wasn't long before the rumor mill was saying that director Robert S was visiting South Woods State Prison. It wasn't unusual for upper level management staff to visit a prison. However, the reason for such a visit was generally known in advance. In this case, no one knew why director Robert S was gracing us with his presence. I was in the middle of a meeting with staff when someone interrupted our meeting to tell me director Robert S was in the front office, and he wanted to see me in the administrator's office immediately.

My meeting with the administrator and director Robert S was brief and to the point. Director Robert S. had complete oversight of the coordinator of chaplaincy services. As such, director Robert S said, "DuBois, you are coming to my office tomorrow morning for an interview." It was well known that director Robert S. was direct and to the point. He didn't even bother with first names or titles. He used your last name—period. It was obvious I was not being asked to report to his office for an interview. I was being directed to report for an interview, and it was not open for debate. It was in my best interest to say, "Yes sir." And with a nod from my administrator, the meeting had ended.

As directed, I presented myself to director Robert S. on the next day, which happened to be a Friday. I knew director Robert S. was considering my appointment as the coordinator of chaplaincy services. I did not know how this interview would proceed. Here's how the interview played out:

Director Robert S said, "DuBois, welcome to Trenton." Then he proceeded to display my letter, which had in effect said thank you but no thanks. Director Robert S then said, "What is this letter all about? Is it loyalty to your administrator?" He then proceeded to tear up my letter and throw it in the trashcan. He then said, "I need your loyalty as well. You report to my office Monday morning as the new coordinator of chaplaincy services."

My reply was simply, "Yes, sir." Thus, my interview was over, and I had just been appointed as the coordinator of chaplaincy services.

I did have one issue to resolve with my new boss. I said, "Director S., I have a previously scheduled training day at the Fairton Federal Correctional Facility on Monday. Would it be okay if I start on Tuesday?"

Director Robert S. said, "No problem, DuBois. You start Tuesday."

On Monday, I did participate in the previously scheduled training at the federal prison. At one point during the training, someone approached me and said, "You have a phone call."

I went to the phone. It was director Robert S. on the line. He said, "DuBois, you passed your first test." With a *bam*...he hung up. He didn't even wait for an answer. He hung up.

On Tuesday, I reported to Trenton as the new coordinator of chaplaincy services. I reported to director Robert S. He said, "DuBois, welcome to central office. Here is your first assignment." He then slid a folder across his desk and said, "Fire this chaplain."

The folder included all the investigative details supporting the firing of a chaplain. I would be expected to deal with the pushback from the ecclesiastical authorities. I knew what needed to be done. I did have one question regarding the phone call. I said, "Director S., I have a question about your phone call and the reference to my first test. What did you mean by a test?"

Director Robert S. simply said, "DuBois, if you tell me you are going to be someplace, that's where you should be. I expect honesty."

To my knowledge, director Robert S. never tested me again. I certainly never gave him reason to doubt my honesty or loyalty.

Over time, director Robert S. and I developed a good working relationship. He was "old school" in many ways. However, I came to know him to be a committed Christian. I was honored to pray with him at a time when he was in the hospital. I was starting to see how God's calling to work was beginning to penetrate the upper levels of a large state department. I hoped to expand on those opportunities. Ultimately, I did have an opportunity to pray with the commissioner and at another time with the chief of staff. These people were the numbers one and two in authority within the Department of Corrections. The work of God's calling in my life included ministry to both the imprisoned and to those responsible for maintaining the prisons.

The Spirit of the Lord God is upon me, because the LORD hath anointed me to preach good tidings unto the meek; he hath sent me to bind up the brokenhearted, to proclaim liberty to the captive, and the opening of the prison to those who are bound. (Isaiah 61:1)

CHAPTER 9

CALLED TO OVERSEE THE CALLED

The coordinator of chaplaincy services provided consultation, support, coordination, and consistency for all religious services in all state facilities. The institutional chaplains provided direct services to staff and to the inmate population at large. In addition, the institutional chaplain served as a liaison between inmates whose faiths are not represented by the institutional chaplain by utilizing the services of volunteers from those specific religious faiths.

The Catholic, Jewish, Protestant, and Islamic faith groups were generally exemplified with institutional chaplains. Representatives of the lesser-populated faith groups required part-time chaplains. As an example, the Native American's inmate population required the part-time services of a tribal leader to construct and oversee the activities related to a sweat lodge. Given this wide range of faith groups, it was not within my authority to evaluate or approve of any one particular

Tenet of their faith. However, I was responsible to ensure that the chaplain or religious volunteer did, in fact, satisfy the religious needs of the inmates in accordance to the basic tenets of their declared faith.

Given this broad description of my oversight responsibilities and the institutional chaplains' role, I still want to remain focused on the calling. The hiring process for a new chaplain required a wide range of coordination with denominational authorities, verification of educational standards, and ordination credentials. The final phase of the hiring process was the interview. During the interview process, I always wanted to explore the concept of a calling. Did the candidate have a clear understanding of their calling to ministry? Some candidates gave a clear description of a calling and with full assurance. Some candidates did not even understand the question. Without identifying any particular faith group, I can only report that, over time, those who had a calling were more effective and responsive to the needs of those under their care. Those who had no concept of a calling were often unresponsive to the needs of others.

CHAPTER 10

CALLED TO RESPOND DURING A CRISIS.

God is our refuge and strength, a very present help in trouble.

—Psalm 46:1

On July 30, 1997, an inmate at Bayside State Prison killed senior corrections officer Frederick W. Baker. This murder created an extremely tense and volatile atmosphere within the prison. The immediate first responders sought to provide aid to the fallen officer, and all efforts were taken to rush the officer to a helipad and transported to a trauma center. All the efforts to save the fallen officer failed.

The prison officials then sought to provide assistance to their first responders. Many of these officers were distraught by the murder and saddened by their failed efforts. In seeking to provide assistance to their staff, the administrative team called upon the services of a local Critical Incident Stress Management (CISM) team. The CISM program had been proven to be effective in walking first responders through a process of normalizing one's response to a traumatic event. CISM teams have been called upon for first responders exposed to the horrors of school shootings, airplane crashes, severe car accidents, tornados, murder scenes, war, and etc. In the call out to a CISM team to assist the first responders in the Baker murder, the good intentions of the prison officials created an additional unexpected trauma. The members of the responding CISM had never been inside a state prison. Under "normal" circumstances, some individuals do not feel comfortable in a prison when the big iron gates clang shut and the sounds of massive locks are engaged. Given the elevated intensity of the atmosphere within the prison, the CISM did what they were called upon to do. However, the experience caused the CISM team to express their immediate trauma concerns in their own debriefing.

Soon after the murder of Officer Fred Baker, I received a phone call from Roland Candle requesting a meeting. Roland was a fireman and head of the local CISM team, which responded to assist the first responders at Bayside State Prison. Roland gave me a compelling reason for the Department of Corrections to create their own CISM team. The primary reason for having a homogeneous team is familiarity. We needed a CISM team where the team members are familiar with the prison setting.

This series of events started a long four-year battle to establish a department-wide CISM team. The battle over the creation of a CISM team involved a series of compromises by administrative staff and union officials. In one sense, it was a typical reaction with one side saying no because the other side is a yes. Then, when you thought things were progressing, the no side said yes and the yes side said no. The final compromise and agreement to proceed was based upon the fact that the department-wide CISM team would be an all-volunteer endeavor. Now the question would be, could we ever get enough civilian and correctional officers to volunteer for a state-wide CISM team? The answer was yes. In July of 2001, four years after the murder of Officer Baker, the Department of Corrections held its first CISM training classes under the instruction of staff from the International Critical Incident Stress Foundation. In addition, I extended an invitation to all chaplains for further training in Pastoral Crisis Intervention. The International Critical Incident Stress Foundation also conducted this training. I was elected as the director for the newly formed all-volunteer Department of Corrections Critical Incident Stress Management (DOC-CISM) team. We initially had approximately fifty team members, which represented a variety of ranking officers and civilian staff.

The first activation for the DOC-CISM team occurred on September 11, 2001. Yes, the tragic events of 9/11 resulted in a call for assistance from the New Jersey Office of Emergency Management. Our new CISM team was called out in support of the New York, New Jersey Port Authority. In reality, we provided support to members of the New York, New Jersey Port Authority; the Fire Department, City of New York (FDNY); the New York Police Department (NYPD); the Federal Bureau of Investigation (FBI); the Red Cross; the US Army; ironworkers; crane operators; dog handlers; and anyone authorized to be working at ground zero in New York City. The New Jersey DOC-CISM team worked in support of the CISM Emergency Management Command Center under the leadership of Roland Candle. We provided direct CISM support for 24/7 for three weeks. This calling surpassed all expectations, and our entire country rallied in response to this tragic event.

On a personal note, I met with Roland Candle for lunch about six months after the events of 9/11. The day after my meeting with

Roland Candle, he passed away. I cannot identify his cause of death; however, I can only imagine it was stress related. In addition, during the height of the 9/11 responses, I had the privilege of having prayer with our commissioner. We often think of being called to a place or to a ministry. However, the calling to meet with individuals also has a place of importance.

CHAPTER 11

CALLED
TO LEAD

And let us not be weary in well doing; for in
due season we shall reap, if we faint not.

—Galatians 6:9

The Department of Corrections gave me a significant promotion and expanded my duties to include oversight of five different offices. I earned the necessary credentials to teach as an instructor to new cadets at the Corrections Officer Training Academy. My promotion as an assistant director, Office of Community Services, allowed me opportunities beyond all expectations. I then had direct oversight over Volunteer Services, Office of Victim Services, county jail inspections, community services (over 110 inmate cleanup details), chaplaincy services, and the initial implementation of a federal grant for the Prison Rape Elimination Act within the NJ DOC. While my new title was that of an assistant director, I did not report to a director. Rather, I reported directly to an assistant commissioner.

I reference these offices as a testament to being called to lead. Competent, qualified, and excellent supervisors were overseeing many of the offices listed under my supervision. I have often thought of the excellence of a winning sports team. The success of a team requires full participation of each member and a coach that allows each team member to exercise their talents to the best of their abilities. Sometimes a good sports team makes their coach look good. I have often thought that my team members made me look good. I was blessed. Hopefully, my leadership contributed to the overall success of the team.

CHAPTER 12

CALLED TO THE RESCUE

My parents made an effort to send my siblings and me to a Christian school. I had the privilege of attending the Vineland Christian School until the fourth grade. At that point in time, a new public elementary school was built just three blocks from our home. I don't know if it was out of convenience or for family financial needs, but I began attending the local public school. Our family and church continued to support the Vineland Christian School. Over the years, the Vineland Christian School switched from a church-sponsored school to a parent-run school. The name was changed to reflect the larger county region and adopted the name Cumberland Christian School (CCS). I had the privilege to teach at the CCS as referenced in chapter six of this book.

From a personal perspective, I had mentioned that my siblings and I were former students in this school. My children attended this school, and my grandchildren were students as well. Interestingly, while I was serving in our first church in the Boston area, Mrs. Gail Haslett taught my children. Later in time, at the Cumberland

Christian School, the same Mrs. Gail Haslett was now teaching my grandchildren.

I had retired as an assistant director from the New Jersey Department of Corrections and was thoroughly enjoying the fact that I didn't need to commute to Trenton any longer. However, it was appearing that another calling was in the making. The Cumberland Christian School was in jeopardy of not making it to its seventieth anniversary. The news around town was that the school was facing a shutdown. In addition, word went out that the headmaster had resigned mid-summer. It was looking like the school was in a freefall collapse. My wife and I had several discussions and mutually felt like God was calling.

Examine me, O LORD, and prove me; test my heart and my mind...that I make known with the voice of thanksgiving, and tell of all thy wondrous works. (Psalms 26:2, 7)

I made an initial call to a former student and friend, Dorothy Pacitto. Dorothy was a member of the CCS board of directors. The details of the school's financial status, decline in enrollment, and overall low morale of staff was depressing. I made an offer to help if the board would be interested. I was a former teacher and middle school principal. I had firsthand knowledge and awareness of the extensive history of the school, and I knew many of the pastors in the surrounding area. I also knew that our enemy would love to see the collapse of such a Christian cornerstone to the region. I was also in a financial position that I didn't need to cause another drain on their finances.

In a matter of days, I received a call from a former student and friend, Heidi Koering. Heidi was the president of the CCS board of directors. After an extensive discussion with Heidi, I was invited to meet with the entire CCS board of directors. After much prayer, and by mutual consent, I was called to serve as the interim headmaster to Cumberland Christian School. I knew this calling was going to be the biggest challenge of my life. I also knew this calling was going to require full use of all my administrative skills. What I didn't know was the extent of future attacks by our enemy against my family and me.

There hath no temptation taken you but such as is common to man; but God is faithful, who will not permit you to be tempted above that ye are able, but will, with the temptation, also make the way to escape, that ye may be able to bear it all. (1 Corinthians 10:13)

I know God will not allow a test beyond our abilities, but I also wanted to be assured that I remained within His calling. As the new interim headmaster, I needed to meet with all of the administrative staff and teaching staff individually and quickly. Linda Grover was my administrative assistant. Linda was super-organized and had the ability to anticipate and prepare for the next hurdle. Linda left before the school year had ended. I was fortunate to then have Debbie Wittie accept the position of administrative assistant with very little training in the position. Debbie quickly adapted to a challenging position with grace and expertise. Margaret Wayman became a valuable all-around help in times of need. Larry Bartlett was the financial director. Sara B. was a lifelong friend. Sara B. willingly served as the elementary school principal and kindergarten teacher. Mark Gebhardt accepted additional duties as a part-time high school principal. Jennie Smith willingly took on addition duties as a part-time middle school principal. I will not list all the other administrative staff and teaching staff, but the dedication of all staff and board members comprised an amazing workforce. However, there needed to be some healing, some assurance, and a tremendous amount of positive leadership.

The immediate concern for the school was the need to hire some teachers. It was getting close to the end of the summer break, and available candidates were difficult to find. There were also some staffing issues which I do not feel comfortable discussing. However, I will say that we actually saw God at work in providing the needed staffing, even up to the day before school opened. The fact that school opened on time and fully staffed was an initial success.

The poor financial condition of the school was alarming. The reduction in enrollment certainly was a contributing factor. However, there were clearly other factors that contributed to a low level of cash flow. I was working with a dire prediction that we would not be able to make payroll by December. There were even some discussions on how or when the school should close. I felt it was important to have a membership meeting prior to the Christmas break and let the entire school family know exactly what we were actually up against. Some did not agree and felt that some parents would get nervous and pre-maturely pull their students out of school over the Christmas break. Yes, a couple of families did. However, the meeting went well, and there was a genuine feeling that we could overcome. In my mind, this all-school family meeting was the second major turn...in the right direction.

Our second major accomplishment at the school was met with a personal setback in my family. On Christmas Eve, my wife received the life-changing diagnosis of breast cancer. Chris would need to have surgery immediately. I was still serving as a pastor and now interim headmaster, so I needed to adjust my time allocation to give the needed critical support to my wife.

The school finances were beginning to improve due to dona-tions and budget adjustments. We were successful in making the payroll. We began planning a large seventieth anniversary banquet. We invited staff, alumni, school families, and church leaders to our banquet. We planned to acknowledge prominent persons, who, over the years, had a positive impact upon the school. We had churches buy tickets for entire tables. We had students create their own fund-raising activities. We had families buying tickets in support of the designated honorees. We had two female students plan an entire father-and-daughter event with all the proceeds going to the school. The entire seventieth anniversary banquet was a success and raised a tremendous amount of money. The school board was beginning to develop a budget for the next year. The mood changed to reflect a more positive thinking for the future.

Our third major accomplishment at the school was again met with a personal setback in my family. In late January, I received the phone call that no parent ever wants to receive. My adult younger son was involved in a very serious automobile accident, and he was being airlifted to the Atlantic City Trauma Center. I cannot discuss much about the accident given the fact that there was a fatality and there continues to be litigation. My son was a passenger, and this was a work-related accident. I would like to focus on two issues related to my family. Upon our arrival at the trauma center, we were told that our son suffered, among other things, severe trauma to the face. We called upon all family, friends, school, and churches seeking prayer for our son. Around 2:00 a.m., we were told our son's vital signs had stabilized. The trauma team leader later told us that, initially, they didn't think our son was going to make it. If this event wasn't traumatic enough, while standing by our son's gurney in the trauma center, my wife received a phone call from her doctor. She was advised that she would need to begin chemo treatments immediately. We had to totally depend upon God to see us through these trying times.

The school board of directors began making plans to hire a new headmaster. It was exciting because plans were being developed to move ahead in preparing for the next school year. There was less concern about defaulting on the payroll. I had only committed to a one-year interim term. (I probably would have stayed another year, but I didn't want the board of directors to rely on that possibility.) The search team for a new headmaster was able to narrow down the field to three possible candidates. The final and most likely candidate, Ken Howard, was available to start before the end of the school year. I liked the idea that the new headmaster could start before the end of the school year. He could be involved in the end-of-the-year graduation ceremonies and give a sense of hope for the future.

Again, with success experienced at the school, I had another family setback. This time, it was my turn. I began to have a problem with my right eye. I called my eye doctor on a Friday evening. I explained my symptoms, and he said to come into his office the next day. During my examination, the doctor confirmed that I had experienced a detached retina. This condition requires immediate surgery to save the eyesight. The doctor was unable to schedule surgery that day. He then scheduled the surgery for Sunday morning. That Sunday happened to be Palm Sunday. When I arrived at the hospital on Palm Sunday, it became clear my doctor had assembled the entire staff necessary for the only surgery scheduled that day—mine. I felt comfortable that all things would work for good.

The end of the school year was a joyful occasion. Headmaster Ken Howard and I both participated in the high school graduation ceremony. The atmosphere was positive with expectations for a successful new school year. I was asked to give the commencement address, and I was given the honor to present the high school diploma to two of my grandsons. God was faithful!

It's been three years since I was called to be the interim headmaster at Cumberland Christian School. The school has had some difficulties due to the Coronavirus pandemic, but it continues to fulfill its overall vital mission. On a personal note, my wife is a cancer survivor, my son is alive, retired, and well with a complete reconstruction of his face, and my eyesight is great. God called us to work, and without a doubt, this was a successful assignment because many people sought to bring praise to God. All praise to God!

The following is how Heidi Koering describes her calling as the board president to the Cumberland Christian School:

> God was laying the foundation for my next step
> in life as I answered the call in 2009 to run for
> the CCS school board, my alma mater. Two years

later, my world turned upside down when my partnership in my father's business ended. My church offered me a position to work part-time in the church office. I accepted the job as I was broken over the ending of my career in the family business and I needed a healthy environment to work. This was a blow to me going from business owner to administrative assistant (which some still called "secretary"). What I did not realize at first was God was preparing me to be available for the next role He had for me. I served CCS on the board for nine years, serving as president many of those years. These were not just typical nine years; they were years of great transition. Within a five-year period, we had four different headmasters. Transition was necessary, and for some, transition is feared and difficult. I, on the other hand, welcome change, as it provides an opportunity for improvement. It was an honor for God to use me to be part of the process as the school now has stabilized and is moving forward.

Jim offered to step in as an interim headmaster; he was a blessing to work with in the leadership of the school. I still remember the day I received the call that he was willing to be interim headmaster for a year to allow the board time to find the right person. He led by example, and he had a gift for bringing people together. It was a year of great healing for the school. We had the privilege of planning the school's seventieth anniversary, which was an awesome interweaving of generations that Jim and I represented. Reflecting back, I still remember Jim as my middle school principal and geography teacher.

CHAPTER 13

CALLED TO
ESTABLISH
A CHURCH

Take heed, therefore, unto yourselves, and to all the flock, over
which the Holy Spirit hath made you overseers, to feed the
church of God, which he hath purchased with His own blood.

—Acts 20:28

In my mind, I never had a goal or even any interest in starting
a church. When I felt my work in my second church was completed, I was comfortable in continuing to serve in the state prison

ministry. However, I began hearing some muttering about churches in our area. Some friends began to propose the idea of starting a new church. I only began considering the idea after my wife and I began attending churches in our area. Something became clear. For many churches in our area, biblical preaching was weak, church music had become anemic, and entertainment had supplanted worship. To further explore the idea of starting a new church, my wife and I invited a group of people to our home. Our group had an open discussion about churches in our area. I didn't want the discussion to just be negative. I tried to see if there was any one church in our area where we would all feel comfortable in supporting. Not a perfect church, just someplace where we could contribute, grow, and worship. We did not identify any one church. The group all sat in a large circle in our living room, and I asked if we could go around the circle and each person give their testimony. We had a more meaningful time of worship in our living room than we had in the past several weeks of church hopping. We then began exploring the idea of starting a new church.

The early days of worship began in our living room. Sunday mornings were a little busy. I had to shift furniture, vacuum, set up chairs, take out the trash, preach, and then put the living room back to its original condition. Fortunately, we had a piano in our living room, and one of our church members, Susan Muller, is a fantastic musician.

Over a period of time, our church grew. We moved from our living room to a couple of different rented facilities. Finally, we purchased an abandoned rescue squad building and converted it into a spiritual rescue and worship building. The calling to my third church resulted in a twenty-seven year assignment.

This is a true saying, If a man desire the office of a bishop, he desireth a good work. (1 Timothy 3:1)

One of our church members, Lee Harrison, felt the calling of God as a minister. Lee completed his graduate level studies at a distinguished seminary. I suggested that Lee develop a comprehensive personal doctrinal statement in preparation for his ordination. It was suggested by someone that Lee should develop his doctrinal statement and present it as a study on Sunday nights. The entire process was beneficial to all, and the doctrinal study became, in part, the overall statement of faith for the church.

Lee and Judy Harrison currently live in Tennessee. Lee serves in the National Guard and pastors a local church in their hometown.

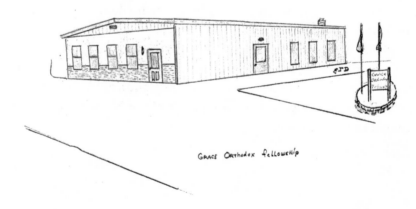

Grace Orthodox Fellowship

CHAPTER 14

CALLED TO A TEAM OF WORKERS

In seeking to address the theme of a calling to work, I tried to highlight my experiences and the callings associated with each specific ministry. In my home church, West Baptist Tabernacle, I was one of three men called to the ministry. Rev. Dale Bossley and Rev. E.M. were the other two called to work from my home church. They have both served in their respective ministries for a number of years.

The following is how Rev. Dale Bossley describes his calling:

> I thank and praise God that I was brought up in a loving Christian home and atmosphere. Not only were my immediate family born again, but my grandparents and many aunts, uncles, and cousins were saved as well. I therefore had the proper

guidance and example constantly before me, and I was accustomed to going to Sunday school and church.

Although my family attended church services and was strict in convictions and discipline, I was not saved until I was eleven. It was on October 17, 1961, at a roller-skating rink in Newburgh, New York, where a state trooper spoke at a Youth For Christ rally. It was at that time that God drew me to Himself. Because of God's grace, I realized what spiritual condition I was in. The truths of the Savior and salvation were presented, and I was caused to repent and believe upon Jesus Christ as my Lord and Savior.

Later, when I was in eighth grade in Jeffersonville, New York, I realized God wanted me in the ministry. I had completed an assignment in which I was to choose a vocation and do research concerning it. A few weeks later, I received a letter from a Christian friend of which the Lord used for me to realize that He wanted me in the gospel ministry, particularly the pastorate. Without hesitation or question, I accepted and desired the work God had for me.

Dale Bossley has served as a pastor of Lows Corners Baptist Church, Grahmsville, New York, for five years; Maranatha Bible Church (Fundamental Baptist), Mountainville, New York, for thirty years; and associate pastor of Cornwall Baptist Church, Cornwall, New York, for three years.

In my first church calling, we were honored to commission someone as a missionary. In my second church, we witnessed the calling of John Shipley as a pastor. In my third church, we ordained Lee Harrison as a pastor. In my brief experience with the Cumberland Christian School, we were privileged to see the calling of several students. Tracy (Hill) Mcworter is now serving as a missionary. Greg H.

is serving as a lead pastor. The prison ministry witnessed the calling of an inmate as a pastor. In addition, senior corrections officer Chuck Serbeck is now serving as a pastor.

Another student, Mark Gebhardt, from Cumberland Christian School, was called by God to serve as a teacher and guidance counselor to the Cumberland Christian School. Mark has also accepted a calling to serve as a pastor. Actually, Mark has taken over as pastor to the church that began in my living room.

I look at these callings as part of the greater calling to His team. My initial experiences in life as a member of a team goes back to those early years of playing football and basketball. My military experiences established the deep understanding that success, or victory, is dependent upon a total team effort. The body of Christ is easily described and understood as the perfectly functioning parts of the entire human body. The eye is important, but the body is not all eyes. The foot and toes are vital, but the body is not all toes. God calls the members of His team as needed to fulfill His plans.

> For by him were all things created, that are in heaven, and that are in earth, visible and invisible, whether they be thrones, or dominions, or principalities or powers—all things were created by him, and for him; And he is before all things, and by him all things consist. And he is the head of the body, the church; who is the beginning, the first-born from the dead, that in all things he might have pre-eminence. (Colossians 1: 16–18)

CHAPTER 15

CALLED BY NAME

T he basis of any calling to work requires the key element of a personal relationship with the God of our salvation.

God is faithful, by whom ye were called unto the fellowship of his Son, Jesus Christ our Lord. (1 Corinthians 1:9)

The work of God can be explored in the greater themes of creation, or judgment, or salvation. However, these (and other) greater themes are paramount when personally experienced. Charles Haddon Spurgeon, in his sermon entitled "God Pleading for Saints and Saints Pleading for God," said, "There is no true understanding of the truths of God except by a personal experience of them." In this sermon, Spurgeon tells of a teaching experience:

> That eminent Puritan preacher, Mr. Thomas Dolittle, was once teaching the catechism to the children of the congregation, as was the wont of the Puritans on the Sabbath day; he came to the question, "What is effectual calling?" The answer was given, as it stands in our admirable catechism, "Effectual calling is the work of God's Spirit, whereby, convicting us of our sin and misery, enlightening our minds in the knowledge of Christ, and renewing our wills, He doth persuade and enable us to embrace Jesus Christ freely offered to us in the gospel." The good man stopped, and said to the lads around him, "Let's use the personal pronoun in the singular; are there any among you who can say that all this is yours?" To his great joy, there stood up one who with many tears and sobs, said, "Effectual calling is the work of God's Spirit, whereby, convicting me of my sin and misery, enlightening my mind in the knowledge of Christ, and the renewing of my will, He hath persuaded and enabled me to embrace Jesus Christ freely offered to me in the gospel." ("God Pleading for Saints and Saints Pleading for God" by Charles Haddon Spurgeon, July 10, 1864, sermon no. 579, Metropolitan Tabernacle Pulpit, Volume 10)

But, now, thus saith the Lord who created thee, O Jacob, and he who formed thee, O Israel, Fear not: for I have redeemed thee, I have called thee by thy name; thou art mine. (Isaiah 43:1)

Even every one who is called by my name; for I have created him for my glory; I have formed him; yea, I have made him. (Isaiah 43:7)

The work of God in creation is often thought of in terms of the great outdoors, the beauty of the mountains, the amazing skies, the beauty of the flowers, and creatures who occupy the depths of the seas. However, consider the fact that God created *you*! His work of creation included you for His glory. His work of salvation for you is designed to manifest His grace.

But God, who is rich in mercy, for his great love with which he loved us, even when we were dead in sins, hath quickened us (made us alive) together with Christ (by grace ye are saved), and hath raised us up together in heavenly places in

Christ Jesus; that in the ages to come he might show the exceeding riches of his grace in his kindness toward us through Christ Jesus, For by grace are ye saved through faith; and that not of yourselves, it is the gift of God—Not of works, lest any man should boast. For we are his workmanship, created in Christ Jesus unto good works, which God hath before ordained that we should walk in them. (Ephesians 2:4–10)

It's fascinating to consider that God's work "quickened us" or "made us alive" that we might demonstrate the exceeding greatness of His grace. The introduction of grace means this salvation is not something we deserve. Neither is it something we can earn. Our salvation is by grace through faith. This process results in our being His workmanship and created unto good works, which God ordained that we should walk.

These facts help to clarify the theme of this book. Called to work highlights the outcomes associated with the purpose of His calling.

And we know that all things work together for good to them that love God, to them who are the called according to his purpose. For whom he did foreknow, he also did predestinate to be conformed to the image of his Son, that he might be the firstborn, that he might be the firstborn among many brethren. Moreover, whom he did predestinate, them he also called; and whom he called, them he also justified; and whom he justified, them he also glorified. (Romans 8: 28–30)

It would appear that God's work is nothing less than amazing. That's why, as Christians, we rejoice in singing the old time hymn "Amazing Grace." It certainly does have a sweet sound.

One thing I know, that, whereas I was blind, now I see. (John 9: 25)

Let's wrap up this chapter with the basic foundation of God's calling to salvation.

Moreover, brethren, I declare unto you the gospel which I preached unto you, which also ye have received, and in which ye stand; by which also ye are saved, if you keep in memory what I preached unto you, unless ye have believed in vain. For I delivered unto you first, that Christ died for our sins according to the scriptures; and that he was buried, and that he rose again the third day according to the scriptures. (1 Corinthians 15: 1–4)

And when the Gentiles heard this, they were glad, and glorified the word of the Lord; and as many as were ordained to eternal life believed. (Acts 13:48)

The work of God in salvation is a great demonstration of His love. I was blessed to have been raised in a Christian home and was expected to attend church on a regular basis as part of our family traditions. On one particular Sunday, at the West Baptist Tabernacle, Vineland, New Jersey, Mr. Kenneth Scheeler presented me with the facts of the Gospel, God gave me an understanding of His Truth, and I believed. All praise and glory go to God alone.

CHAPTER 16

CALLED TO ASSURANCE

The assurance of salvation is based on the work of God and with the understanding that nothing can separate us from the love of God (Romans 8:35–39).

> Yea, before the day was, I am he; and there is none that can deliver out of my hand; I will work and who shall hinder it? (Isaiah 43:13)

These passages give us the assurance that no one can alter or delay or in any way hinder the work of God. Therefore, His calling to work is entirely based upon His work.

My mother, Dorothy M. DuBois, was a loving Christian and a well-respected Sunday school teacher. When I was in Bible college I would come home and ask her questions about the new things I was learning. Mom always seemed to be familiar with even some of the most complex theological issues. From a human perspective, my mother was a rock. However, she firmly believed in the LORD as her Rock. The following is a poem (song) written by my mother:

The Rock Is My Dwelling Place

On shifting sands I have not built,
Secure and safe I'll be.
Protection from life's fierce storms,
Has been my Redeemers' decree.
For;
The Rock is my dwelling place,
Of this I will sing.
The Rock is my hiding place,
To this I will cling.

Water from the Rock, I drink,
Pure, cold, and delightful to me.
My thirst is quenched. I'm happy and content,
For-ever and eternally.
For;
The Rock is my dwelling place,
Of this I will sing.
The Rock is my hiding place,
To this I will cling.

I will sing from the Rock a song of love,
Pardon, and salvation free.
For Jesus is the Blessed Rock,
All this He gave to me.

For;
The Rock is my dwelling place,
Of this I will sing
The Rock is my hiding place,
To this I will cling.

Dorothy M. DuBois, July 28, 1946

The following is a musical composition of "The Rock Is My Dwelling Place" by my mother's great-grandchildren, Joshua and Jacob DuBois: Copyright © 2021

The Rock is My Dwelling Place

Poem by: Dorothy M. DuBois- July 28, 1946   Composed by: Joshua and Jacob DuBois

CHAPTER 17

CALLED TO EQUIP THE SAINTS FOR THE WORK

I recall a period of time in the ministry when I was having some particular difficulties. Several people, trying to be encouraging, kept saying to me, "Be not weary in well doing." For some reason, the words intended as encouragement fell short. For some reason the words of encouragement sounded hollow. Finally, I turned to the verses in the Bible and found that my "well-wishers" were not quoting the complete sentence. The missing yet important words were the exclusion of the "let us" and the "we."

And let us not be weary in well doing; for in due season we shall reap, if we faint not. (Galatians 6:9)

The concept of being called to work is both a personal and a collective calling. The calling of a pastor is for the perfecting of the church for the work of the ministry. Let us be not weary in the work. Let us do the work of the ministry. Let us work together. Let us reap the outcomes together. I recall a time when someone called me and asked if I would visit someone. At the time, I was thinking, *Why don't you* (the caller) *visit with the person in need?* Obviously, God had placed the person in need upon the heart of the caller. Sure, there are times when the pastor should visit with those in need. However, we all have a vital part in the ministry. If God lays the needs of someone upon your heart, perhaps you are the best person to meet those needs. Let us not be weary in meeting the needs of others.

And he gave some, apostles; and some, prophets; and some, evangelists; and some, pastors and teachers; For the perfecting of the saints for the work of the ministry for the edifying of the body of Christ, Till we all come to the unity of the faith, and the knowledge of the Son of God, unto a perfect man, unto the measure of the stature of the fullness of Christ; That we henceforth be no more children, tossed to and fro and carried

about with every wind of doctrine, by the sleight
of men, and cunning craftiness, by which they lie
in wait to deceive. (Ephesians 4:11–14)

I love to see how the apostle Paul outlined the expected outcomes for evangelists, and pastors, teachers.

- The perfecting of the saints for the work of the ministry.
- The edifying of the body of Christ.
- Pursuing unity of the faith.
- Pursuing knowledge of the Son of God.
- Seeking the measurable prominence of the fullness of Christ.
- Protecting the body of Christ from false doctrine.

Notice how these expected outcomes do not focus on numbers, budgets, programs, or popularity. If I were asked to summarize these expected outcomes into one word, it would be "maturity." The writer to Hebrews compares the immature as a "babe" with no skillful use of the Word of God. However, the mature Christian applies reason and repeated use of the Word of God to discern between both good and evil. Ultimately, the goal of the pastor-teacher is that of maturity in Christ-likeness within the body of Christ.

CHAPTER 18

CALLED TO BE DISCIPLES

In a very general sense, a disciple is a learner or a student. Yes, we are all expected to put into practice that which we learn. Therefore, Christ-likeness is the outcome of being a follower of Christ. I like the passage of Scripture in John 11:16, wherein Thomas refers to his fellow-disciples. I believe we could easily identify Thomas as a disciple who had to learn some lessons as he followed Christ. As a fellow-disciple, I had to learn some lessons as I followed Christ in the work He called me to do.

As a disciple, I have learned that preaching may have an impact upon the "hearers" of the Word in ways unintended by the preacher. As an example, while I was a student at Philadelphia College of Bible, I was invited to preach at the Atlantic City Rescue Mission, Atlantic City, New Jersey. This would be the first time I would preach a message. I was excited, nervous, and flat-out petrified. I wrote out every word of the message. I studied and prepared and tried to reduce the pages to a manageable outline. I prayed for calmness and clarity in speech. As the day and time arrived for my first message, I was "pleased" to see that the chapel at the rescue mission was packed. I recall it being a cold winter night, and many of the homeless in Atlantic City were seeking refuge. At that time, individuals who sought the services of the rescue mission were all required to attend the evening worship service. I began my sermon and was completely focused on my notes when, to my surprise, someone in the audience interrupted me with a question. My initial thought was, *Hey, you're not supposed to ask a question.* Then I thought, *Hey, that's a really good question.* At that moment, I became less tied to my outline and notes. I answered the question and was able to adjust the sermon to address the needs of the audience.

As a disciple, I learned to appreciate the advice and council of seasoned and mature Christians. This lesson is learned from Psalms 1:1 as "blessed is the man who walketh not in the council of the ungodly." In my first church, I was blessed to learn from Mrs. Grayton. This elderly Christian woman was an example of a prayer warrior and a witness. During those occasions when I visited with Mrs. Grayton, I would come to the end of our visit time together, and I would ask if we could pray together. Before I could finish my comment, Mrs. Grayton would be on her knees and praying for our church ministry and me. I also learned how this physically frail woman would be an active witness. Mrs. Grayton would travel to the mall with her family members. Her family would shop, and Mrs. Grayton would sit on a bench in the mall. She would pray, "Lord, please send someone to sit with me today so that I may witness to him or her and share the Gospel."

As a disciple, I learned that often the main points of my message were less important to some than what I may have considered as major. I have been amazed how often someone would comment on how blessed they were by something in a sermon. I would later reflect on that comment and consider how God used what I considered as a less important point as a blessing.

As a disciple, I learned that sometimes we underestimate the ability of some to understand and apply a message. In our first church, we had members of the church who worked at a local mentally-and-physically-challenged facility. The workers were allowed to bring some of their clients to church. It was a blessing to have these challenged individuals in our worship services. They particularly liked it when we had refreshments or a luncheon after church. Actually, even those less challenged looked forward to the luncheons. During one particular sermon, one of the challenged clients started to cause a disturbance. At the time, I wasn't sure what was going on, but one of the clients was making a point of saying, "No more." Those around him did their best to quiet him down, but he was obviously upset about something. I made sure he was okay and then continued with the sermon.

After church was over, I asked, "What was the problem with the J——?" Apparently, during the message, I was focused on the fruit of the Spirit. I made one comment about not being drunk with wine but, rather, being filled with the Spirit (Ephesians 5:18). The young man who caused the disturbance had celebrated his birthday that week. His family had snuck some wine into his room as part of his birthday celebration. During the church service, he had heard the one comment about wine. He heard and internalized this comment and made a determination that he wanted "no more wine." I learned a lesson to never underestimate the ability of God to use any portion of His Word, even in those who may appear as unable to learn. Indeed, God gives understanding of the Scriptures.

Then opened he their understanding, that they
might understand the scriptures. (Luke 24:45)

As a disciple, I have learned to appreciate the deep spiritual history and experiences of others. When we, as a country, were experiencing the stay-at-home orders to mitigate the effects of the COVID-19 virus pandemic, my wife and I joined with our fellow church members to worship together online each Sunday for a virtual worship experience. In reflection upon this worship experience, I found a similarity to the founders of our first church. Members in our first church were immigrants from the old Russia and Ukraine. I remember some of the elderly church members sharing copies of handwritten Bibles and hymnbooks. These precious documents were written while listening to Christian radio ministries. In a closed society, the Christians worshiped, sang hymns and, in the absence of a Bible or a hymnal, they wrote down the Word and hymns in the privacy of their homes. I trust we, as Christians, can appreciate what others have experienced in their spiritual journey, especially within a closed society.

As a disciple, I have learned what it means to give and to receive. Back in the early years of marriage, my wife and I were not faithful in tithing. You know how that story goes. We couldn't afford to tithe. In reality, we were poor. Well, a relative of mine challenged us in the context of the biblical accounts of not "robbing" God (Malachi 3:8–10). In January of 1972, my wife and I began tithing as a regular part of our giving. At the time, I had a minimum-paying job in a local glass factory. We were expecting our second child, and his due date was around the end of February. My health benefits at work were not very substantial. In fact, the hospital was demanding a hundred-dollar deposit to offset the weakness of my insurance coverage. We didn't have that much money.

I'm sure you know what was on my mind. (If we didn't tithe, we would have had the deposit expected by the hospital.) On the first of March, I was called into the main office at the glass factory. At this point, our son was past due. The company officials were changing my status from an hourly employee to that of a salary employee. The reason for this change of status was simply the fact that the company wanted me to work overtime without getting paid for the overtime. Salary employees were expected to work overtime without any additional pay. My immediate question was related to any potential pay raise. Was I going to receive an increase in my salary? The short answer was no. The longer answer was also a no. However, the only thing that changed was my insurance coverage. Yes, the birth of our son was completely covered under the new insurance coverage. Our son was born seven days after the new coverage took effect. We have never had to second-guess God's sovereignty, and with His blessings, we have been blessed to give above and beyond our wildest expectations.

I have one more lesson to share. When I quit my dream job to attend Bible college, my wife took a job in a local factory. I applied for my veterans' benefits for payment of college expenses. Typically, my veteran benefits took a few months to process. From a financial perspective, this college experience was beginning to look like a disaster. We were falling behind in paying our bills on time. Finally, a week before Christmas, I received my first installment of the much-needed benefits. My wife and I sat down with our pile of outstanding bills. We began writing checks for our church tithe, past-due bills, and borrowed money. The total of all outstanding bills came to the same amount of payment from my veterans' check. The difference was literally within pennies. All bills paid; however, we had zero money for Christmas presents for our two children. When we attended church the Sunday before Christmas, an elderly lady from our church gave us an unexpected gift of $300. From a financial perspective, we witnessed God at work through His people. This experience taught us a lesson. We need to be good stewards of His resources in our lives. We also need to be willing to share with others in times of their needs. I don't know how the lady from church knew we had a need, but we have learned to listen to God's leading and look for ways to help others in their time of needs.

One unique way my wife and I would celebrate our wedding anniversary was to go out for a fancy dinner. At first, you may say going out for dinner is not unique. Yeah, I know. But we would look for another couple and invite them out for dinner with us. Usually, it was another couple that wouldn't necessarily be able to afford a fancy dinner.

CHAPTER 19

CALLED TO BE
A WITNESS

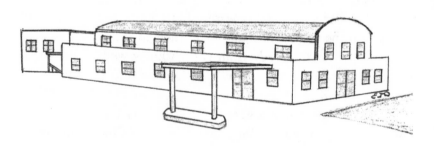

WEST BAPTIST TABERNACLE

I n my early years of childhood, God placed me in an environment of exposure to observe some of His greatest servants. My grandfather was a Methodist minister. He was a genuine "circuit rider" in that he traveled by horseback to preach in several churches in southern New Jersey. It would then be understandable that my father was a true Methodist. My mother, on the other hand, was a true Baptist.

This family dichotomy resulted in my attending services of two different denominations. Actually, I was blessed to witness some of the best preachers in South Jersey.

Pastor Edward Walter Cooper was a dynamic speaker and truly a student of the Bible. He loved to preach and teach from the Old Testament. He established a Baptist church in Vineland, New Jersey. The city of Vineland is the largest town, by area, in New Jersey. The town had a Baptist church on the east side of town. However, the town was divided by a railroad. Pastor Cooper sought to establish a Baptist church on the west side of town so the children didn't need to cross the railroad tracks to attend church. Thus, the original Baptist church on the east side of town adopted the name First Baptist Church. Pastor Cooper established a Baptist church of the west side of town and adopted the name West Baptist Church. The West Baptist Church grew and built a large church and later adopted the name West Baptist Tabernacle. The opening of the West Baptist Tabernacle was packed when Evangelist J.D. Daily and Evangelist Oliver Green were invited to preach. I grew up in the West Baptist Tabernacle under the leadership of Pastor Edward W. Cooper and Pastor Benjamin Taylor and was ultimately ordained in that church.

My life was also influenced by some of the best preachers in southern New Jersey at the Malaga Camp. The Malaga Camp is officially known as the West Jersey Grove Association. While claiming to be a non-denominational organization, the association bylaws calls for the president of the camp to be a Methodist minister. The summer camp meetings have a rich history and are currently celebrating their 152nd year of ministry. I was blessed to live as a year-round resident of Malaga Camp. The camp brought in some of the greatest preachers as guest speakers. However, the camp also had some of the best preachers as part of its leadership.

One of the greatest persons of influence at Malaga Camp was Dr. Norman W. Paullin. Dr. Paullin was a professor at Eastern Baptist College (now Palmer Theological Seminary). The schedule of guest speakers at Malaga Camp typically occupied the first two weeks of August. Dr. Paullin was so popular that the camp extended its summer schedule to give Dr. Paullin his own week, that being the third week of August each year.

Another person of influence was Dr. Even C. Pedrick. Dr. Pedrick was the president of Malaga Camp for many years. He was a great preacher and a leader. He had a tremendous connection to all the pastors of south Jersey. He also served as a chaplain at Leesburg State Prison. Earlier, I wrote about Rev. Paul Pedrick as the chaplain who hired me. Dr. Even Pedrick was his father. This brings up an interesting point of following in the footsteps of a very popular and successful leader. Jane Pedrick recalls how her late husband responded to God's calling for Paul to follow in his father's role as a chaplain at Leesburg State Prison and president of Malaga Camp, as follows:

> In 1974, Rev. Paul W. Pedrick was pastoring West Side United Methodist Church in Millville, New Jersey. He had been there for seven years. During this time, Paul had been struggling for about six months as to whether God was calling him to be a chaplain at Bayside State Prison in Leesburg, New Jersey. His father, Dr. Evan C. Pedrick was the longtime chaplain there. In fact, he was one of the first prison chaplains in the state of New Jersey.
>
> Paul loved his ministry in the church. All was going well at West Side UMC. There was no reason to leave. Paul did not want to just follow in his father's footsteps. He wanted to do God's will. Finally, after six months of praying and struggling and listening for God to make it clear to him, he told the Lord, "If this is Your will, I am willing." He then informed his dad for the first time. His dad was retiring and had never asked Paul to take over or if he was even interested in the position. From that time forth, everything fell into place. This was not a problem for me. I had been going into the prison on Sunday after-

noons since I was thirteen years old. Our church youth group would hold services for the inmates under the direction of Dr. Pedrick. Little did I know at the time what God had in mind. If this was God's calling, then I was all for it.

Paul's prison ministry opened the door to meet with various prison ministries throughout the United States. One such ministry was the Bill Glass Ministries. Bill was a retired football player. He played for the Cleveland Browns. He also received induction into the football hall of fame. The Bill Glass Ministries traveled throughout the United States and Puerto Rico to minister to inmates. He would bring many Christian celebrities to give their testimonies. Paul and I traveled with the team when we could. We were in twenty different states as counselors and coordinators in men and women's prisons. After traveling to so many states, Bill Glass made the statement that the ministry at Bayside State Prison was one of the best in the United States. I have accepted this statement as a confirmation that Paul not only took over a very successful ministry from his father, but he also expanded the ministry into a well-respected ministry from highly respected national leaders in prison ministries. Paul had a very successful ministry at the prison.

Paul loved his ministries. He served as the supervisor of chaplaincy services, part-time pastor of the Port Elizabeth UMC, and president of Malaga Camp Meeting for twenty-seven years. Upon his retirement, Paul joined with the Francis Asbury Society in Wilmore, Kentucky, and served as an evangelist.

Paul's journey in this life came to end with a battle with cancer. During this medical battle,

Paul had approximately two hundred visitors in his home in a two-month period of time. Paul prayed with each of his visitors from his bed at home. Paul's ministry continued to be meaningful even in a difficult time of illness.

(Note: The Bayside State Prison is the same Leesburg State Prison. At a point in time, the state authorities changed the names of all prisons to remove any references to cities or towns in direct connection with state prisons.)

For I know the thoughts that I think toward you, saith the LORD, thoughts of peace, and not of evil, to give you an expected end. (Jeremiah 29:11)

Rev. Archie Shaw was the first chaplain of the Grove Chapel at Malaga Camp. The Grove Chapel was established on the grounds of Malaga Camp as a place of worship for year-round residents of the camp. My father, Charles L. DuBois, physically built the Grove Chapel and participated in the musical ministry at the chapel. The Grove Chapel had some of the best preachers as chaplains and as guest speakers.

During my senior year as a student at Philadelphia College of Bible, I was invited to serve as the chaplain at the Grove Chapel. Every Sunday afternoon, I had the privilege of preaching to a group of mature Christians. Two particular persons who were regular in attendance were Dr. and Mrs. Bustard. Remember her? I mentioned in chapter four that Mrs. Bustard wrote my letter of reference for my first church. Dr. Bustard was a professor at the Reformed Episcopal Seminary in Philadelphia, Pennsylvania. Yes, I was a student in training and preaching to a group of mature Christians. Rest assured, I was motivated to study and carefully prepare each sermon because those in attendance knew their Bible extremely well. In addition, Mrs. Bustard was not bashful about offering her evaluation of any given sermon. This experience was a great learning experience and served to underscore the biblical admonition to study.

Study to show thyself approved unto God, a workman that needeth not to be ashamed, rightly diving the word of truth. (2 Timothy 2:15)

Malaga Camp Tabernacle

CHAPTER 20

CALLED TO VOLUNTEER

M artin Luther King Jr. once said, "Life's most persistent and urgent question is, What are you doing for others?"

It is not hard to see how many people are involved in ministry as volunteers. Look around the local church and count the individuals involved as Sunday school teachers, choir members, worship teams, ushers, sound personnel, counselors, nursery workers, officers, deacons, elders, and even the less seen are the prayer warriors.

Volunteerism Is a Noble Cause

Author Unknown

"If you want to touch the past,
touch a rock.

If you want to touch the present,
touch a flower.

If you want to touch the future,
touch a life."

As every man hath received the gift, even so minister the same one to another, as good stewards of
the manifold grace of God. (1 Peter 4:10)

The late Dorothy Esther Wright was a gifted musician. God
blessed Dorothy with the ability to lead our church choir for a
number of years. It was often humorous when the men in the choir
had some difficulty hitting the proper notes. We would know that
Dorothy Esther would gently, but directly and correctly, zero in on
our mistake(s). God gifted her with an "ear" that could hear the best
in music. One of Dorothy Esther's favorite hymns was "The Family
of God."

Susan Muller is another very gifted musician. Susan's ability to
play the piano falls into the category of highly exceptional and spiritually uplifting. Many, many times when Susan would play special
music during the observance of communion, I (and many others)
were moved to tears.

The following is how Susan Muller describes her calling to a
ministry of music:

> From the time I was four years old, my parents
> noticed that I lovingly touched the keys on my
> grandmother's piano. When I was seven years old,
> I began piano lessons, which continued through
> Bible college at the School of the Bible and Music

in Grand Rapids, Michigan. During my teenage years, the Lord began to give me the desire to serve Him with my music. He began to open up opportunities as I played for our church Sunday school and later travelled in two music groups throughout the Midwest, both singing and playing. For all my adult life (about fifty years), God has blessed me to play in several churches. I am thankful for my parents, who encouraged me to practice daily, and for the three piano teachers who taught me to play the piano. The Lord has blessed me with a ministry for Him, and it is my desire that He uses my playing for His glory.

And the King shall answer and say unto them, Verily, I say unto you, Inasmuch as ye have done it unto one of the least of these my brethren, ye have done it unto me. (Matthew 25:40)

The value of the ministry of volunteers in a prison setting is beyond measure. One of the more progressive ideas in recruiting and managing volunteers was the establishment of a full-time coordinator of volunteers. I was fortunate to have the one and only state prison position of a coordinator of volunteers. This position was established to provide a volunteer force meeting the needs of over three thousand incarcerated individuals. When you consider my concern for hiring chaplains with a clear sense of a calling by God, you can imagine how critical it would be to have the coordinator of volunteers who would themselves be sensitive to their own calling.

The following is how Carol Malone describes God's leading in her being hired as the coordinator of volunteers at South Woods State Prison:

I was raised in a Christian home and attended a Christian church that taught me as a teen to pray about *every* aspect of my future, including my husband–to-be, my career, my home, etc. This was reinforced by the scripture found in Jeremiah 29:11, "For I know the plans I have for you, declares the Lord, plans to prosper you and not to harm you, plans to give you hope and *a future*." It should have come as no surprise then when God really did answer my prayers and guided me each step of the way in all these areas. I am specifically going to share about the "calling" that God had in store for my life.

My own career plan was that I attended college and earned my bachelor's degree in elementary education. I taught full time for nine years at a private Christian school before having children, and then I worked part time at a private preschool for another five years after having my two sons. It was when both of my boys became school age that I desired to return back to full-time work so that I could contribute to paying school tuition for the Christian education that I desired for them.

Despite my efforts to apply and interview for many different types of jobs within the private and public sector, in-school and out-of-school settings, I came up empty handed. These repeated rejections were very difficult for me as I felt that I was a worthy candidate for all of them. It began to affect my self-esteem when I could not even snag jobs that I felt I was overqualified for. It was during this time that I cried out to God that nothing seemed to be a fit for me and could He just "create" a job just for me if He had to.

Shortly thereafter, an individual at church gave me a booklet and said that a new prison was going to be built and they would be hiring a lot of people, in case I was interested. This person did not even know that I was seeking full-time employment and that I was becoming discouraged on my quest. I thought, *Could this booklet that was literally placed into my hands be an answer to prayer from God?* I immediately became excited at this new prospect and felt a leading in this direction.

I reflected back to when I was a child of about ten years old. I had been drawn to listen to the radio every Saturday morning to a program called *Chaplain Ray*, who was a prison chaplain. At the time, I was really impressed and intrigued by it. Strange activity for a little girl, I admit. I have no idea how I came across the program. I probably just stumbled upon it, *or* did God, by some "coincidence," have it cross my path in preparation for my future? For whatever reason, at the time, this radio program piqued my interest. I then reflected on how my husband and I had been volunteering through my church at various county, state, and federal prisons in our area. We loved presenting the Gospel through music, and I had been assisting the head of our church's prison ministry team by creating schedules for the volunteers. I had a heart for the inmates.

Needless to say, I quickly poured over all the alphabetized job titles and descriptions in the booklet. The *very* last position in the booklet was for a volunteer services assistant. The description sounded like some things that I had already been doing. I felt excited about the prospect of doing something that I love that would be a ministry unto the Lord. To *get paid* for doing it? How unbelievable would that be? I completed the interest form and mailed it right out.

Long months went by. Finally, a postcard came to see if I was still interested in the position. If so, I needed to take the Civil Service Exam. It was close to a year since I had filled out my interest card, so things were moving very slowly. I responded back. Finally, I got another postcard to announce the testing at the Vineland High School cafeteria that December for *the exam.* Nerves set in. I hadn't taken any kind of major test in at least a decade since I was in college.

I remember my mom and aunt prayed for me that Saturday morning before I left to take the test. I didn't want to take it, yet I felt compelled to do so. I entered the large cafeteria, and they had us sit a seat apart from each other, and the place was *full.* I asked those around me why they were there, what they were testing for. My heart sank as I heard them all say they were there to test for the volunteer services position. I soon realized that they were *all* there for this *one* position. I felt like I was going to be sick to my stomach when I thought, unlike the correction officers position where *hundreds* of people will be hired, there is only *one* volunteer services position, and a hundred people are here who want it. Panic and fear began to set in, and I questioned myself, What was I doing there? Who did I think I was that I could "win" out over this crowd of applicants? Why was I setting myself up for more failure and rejection after I had been turned down for so many other jobs? I would certainly rather be out Christmas shopping than here!

When the test began, I could hardly think or comprehend it. Before long, I began to notice that people around me were turning their tests in. That brought a new wave of disorientation and panic to my mind because I was nowhere near being finished. I had never felt such anxiety and stress over a test in my entire life. My heart was starting to beat out of my chest!

I stopped dead in my tracks and *prayed* to calm myself down. Very vividly, I recall how I felt exactly like the spies who gave a negative report on the Promised Land that God was giving to them. I felt like I was in the land of giants and that I was a little insignificant grasshopper getting ready to be stepped on and squashed. When that Bible story became a reality in my spirit, something rose up inside of me, and I said to myself, "I am *not* a grasshopper, and I have just as much right to be here as they do. I serve the God of the universe, and He is all knowing, and He knows the answer to all these questions." So I asked God to please help me! I found a new calmness and assurance from God, and I went back and changed some answers and turned it in.

In mid-spring, the results came back that I scored in fourth place of all those tested. I could *not* believe it! *Praise God!* That was quite a journey, but now it had ended because they would be interviewing only the top three candidates for the position.

In early summer, my husband, two sons, and I were on a vacation at a theme park in Virginia. My husband took my oldest son on one of the roller-coaster rides that went forwards and then backwards. The backward trek was so abrupt my husband did not get a chance to brace himself and he hurt his back. He was in such pain that we had to leave the park and go home immediately.

When we arrived home, there was a message left on my telephone answering machine. This was way before there were cell phones and texting and such. The message was for me and stated that one of the top three scorers for the volunteer services assistant position had backed out. Since I was the fourth-highest scorer, I was the next person on the list to be considered for a job interview and that I was to call them back within twenty-four to forty-eight hours. If I didn't respond back, they would take that to mean that I was no longer interested and they would proceed to contact the next eligible person.

I could *not* believe this turn of events! I had already mentally closed the door of being considered and had not thought any more about it. I called immediately and was set up for an interview appointment. If we had *not* come home immediately when we did, that opportunity would have passed right on by. Was it some coincidence that my husband insisted that we leave our vacation and come home as soon as possible? I think it was more of a God-incidence than a coincidence.

The interview was held inside the prison, I assume, to see if the individuals being considered for the position felt comfortable going through security and being inside the environment where the inmates would be walking about. No sweat for me. I was used to going in and out of the other prisons where I had volunteered. It didn't bother me a bit.

The individual that was supposed to interview me was not available that day, and so another person was set up. This person was none other than the chaplaincy supervisor, Rev. E. James DuBois. We had what I considered to be a *great* interview. He made me feel very comfortable, and I shared my background, experiences, and my activities at other prisons and how comfortable I felt on the "inside" due to my volunteer work. The fact that I had been on numerous interviews in the past year, without seeming success, gave me something to draw from and put me at ease.

Within days, I was offered the position, and I began work on Monday August 4, 1997. I settled into my position, and I absolutely loved it and felt this was where I would be for the remainder of my working days. I finally arrived at what God had called me to do. I always felt extremely fortunate to do something that I loved. I never referred to my career at the NJDOC as simply a job but, rather, as a ministry as unto the Lord, and I am extremely blessed to be paid for doing it.

Another very interesting thing came to light for me as I met with others in my department at a staff meeting one day. One social worker mentioned to me that she had also applied for my position and had taken the test for it in Hammonton. Another social worker said she had tested for it also, but in Atlantic City. I was completely astounded at these revelations. Not only did God honor me to score higher than those in my testing room at Vineland High but also in two other locations on different dates. Also, I marveled at how I was assigned to test at Vineland High School, a place that I was familiar with because I had taken a few courses there as a satellite unit from my college. Being uncomfortable to drive myself outside of the county, I may not have even gone to take the exam if I had been assigned to either one of these other testing areas.

Wow, my God is an Awesome God! He has proven himself over and over to me and had prepared my path all along the way to get me to this place. I knew that I had a calling on my life, and God took me step by step to arrive at the place where he wanted me to be. First, to listen to Chaplain Ray in my childhood, to prepare me by calling me to volunteer in prisons where I had developed a comfort factor already, to prepare me for some aspects of the job description by my organizing schedules for my church, to be handed the booklet that advertised the prison, to assign me to a familiar testing location, to answer my prayers and those of supportive family members when I took the Civil Service Exam, to enable me to score high enough to be at the top of the list (*all* praise to God on that one especially), to get me home from a family vacation in another state to receive the phone call in time, to provide prior opportunities for me to gain interviewing skills, and to assist me during *the* interview. I sincerely believe that God did "create" this job just for me too, as this was indeed a unique position—no other prison had it. I was the only person in the entire New Jersey Department of Corrections that had this title.

I always told people that I felt like Queen Esther in the Bible for such a time as this. God placed me in the newest and largest state prison in New Jersey to specifically bring light into a dark world. The harvest is ripe because when you are at the very lowest place in your life, there is no other place to look but up. That is the situation that many of these men find themselves in when they arrive. They are alone, abandoned, despised by family and society, guilt-ridden, and ashamed of their actions that brought them to this place.

I have been so privileged for the past twenty-three years to have had the opportunity to serve as the volunteer services assistant at South Woods State Prison to enable many different churches to come inside these walls to bring the uncompromising Word of God to those that need it the most. I have met so many wonderful Christian volunteers over these years, some of which have already gone on to be with the Lord, and whom I look forward to meeting once again on heavenly shores.

God did have plans to prosper me and to give me a future, and He will do the same for you if you will trust Him with your life.

The Bible guides us to "trust in the Lord with all thine heart; and lean not unto thine own understanding. In all thy ways acknowledge him, and he shall direct thy paths" (Proverbs 3:5–6). Psalm 37:4 states, "Delight thyself also in the Lord: and He shall give thee the desires of thine heart." Just trust and obey.

As He did with my career, God brought me an awesome husband whom I have been married to for over four decades. God also blessed me with two wonderful sons, daughters-in-law, a granddaughter, and I am living in the house of

my dreams! He has truly given me *all* the desires
of my heart!

I love how Carol describes the timing of some events as "more
of a God-incidence than a coincidence." I have had many "God incidents," and the timing of events or encounters cannot be explained
in any manner of my coordination. I would like to share another case
of a "God incident." As the director of the volunteer NJ DOC CISM
team, I received a call concerning an attempted suicide by one of our
correctional officers. Under normal circumstances, I would seek to
find a volunteer CISM team member who could respond to this call.
I didn't seek to find an available CISM team member. I just took the
call myself and proceeded to meet with the officer. Our initial efforts
resulted in the officer being taken to a hospital. When I arrived at
the hospital, I saw a man of a different race, yet of my same age, in
crisis. The officer was in civilian clothing and was wearing a shirt
identifying his affinity for the army. I used our mutual regard for the
army and sought to establish something we may have had in common. As it turned out, this officer and I served in Vietnam, in the
same aviation unit, at the same time. The officer was in a place where
he was being provided the necessary medical assistance. Our mutual
connection provided a personal level of concern and compassion. I
did not consider this encounter as a coincidence. It was one of many
"God incidents."

For we are his workmanship, created in Christ
Jesus unto good works, which God hath before
ordained that we should walk in them. (Ephesians
2:10)

While we are in the midst of a discussion on volunteerism and "God incidents," I am excited to share with you the testimony of a prison chaplain who, like me, started as a volunteer. His calling to prison ministry was uniquely a leading by God. The following is the testimony of Chaplain William Cawman in an article he wrote for this book.

Who Can Know the Mind of the Lord?

The thought of becoming a state prison chaplain would have been the remotest of ambitions for the first half century of my life. I graduated from theological seminary and then taught in a Christian school for about ten years, after which I worked as a construction superintendent for a commercial contractor for almost eighteen years. I had no idea that such was all a preparation for the further calling God had upon my life. But even though we mortals have to keep on learning that God knows what He is doing, He keeps right on knowing it.

In 1994, I was running some good-size construction projects and enjoying it, knowing that, at the time, I was where God wanted me to be. But that year, an account came out in our local newspaper of what the police department labeled the "most heinous murder they had ever witnessed." Three young boys—one seventeen and two sixteen—had broken into the home of an elderly couple and brutally murdered them down in cold blood, walking off with $37 for the atrocity.

As I read of the account in the news, something began to haunt my inner being. Yes, there were two innocent victims taken out for such senseless criminality, but also, I began to hurt for three young victims of our society. What could ever cause three young lives to become so misdirected as this? I could not shake off the feeling about it; I couldn't lay the matter down and forget it. Finally, I called the county court and asked about them. They told me they had been turned over to the state, and they gave me the prison locations of two of them. They could not find the third.

I wrote a letter to each of the two they had given me the addresses for. The first letter returned was from the seventeen year old. His opening words were: "First of all, I want to thank you for caring about me." My heart was moved as I began to learn the answer to my nagging question, "What went so wrong?" How would I feel—what would my life have been—if no one had ever cared for me? He invited me to visit him and put me on his visit list. I did so, and I believe the Lord really saved him. The second boy responded with these words: "If I knew more about you, I would tell you more about me." When he found that I was visiting the first boy, he wrote back and said, "If you are visiting him, I don't want anything to do with you—ever!" Nine years later, I received a letter from him asking me to forgive him and that he would like to correspond with me.

The first boy told me the location of the one no one could tell me about. I wrote to him but heard nothing back but continued to write for about a year. Finally, he wrote back to me and asked if I would come see him. He was imprisoned in a maximum-security prison for sixty years without parole. As I entered the visit hall not knowing what he would look like or how we would recognize each other, both of us headed for each other, don't ask me how. We sat down, and he said, "I want to ask you a question, but first of all, let me tell you something. When you first wrote to me, I did not answer you because I felt it was too good to be true. No one cares about me. But when you continued to write, I thought, Why don't I give him a try? What do I have to lose? My question is, Why did you write to me?"

I told him that when I read about him, my heart was burdened for him and I cared about him. He told me he had been born in a military camp and really did not know his father. He had moved all around and ran with gangs in Miami Beach and Vineland. At the age of sixteen, he was sick and tired of such a life and said to his gang leader, "I'm sick and tired of this." His gang leader said he was too. One week later, they broke into the home and committed the crime.

He was sent to prison, and shortly thereafter, someone told him that if he wanted God to forgive him, He would, but he would have to ask Him to. That night, after his cellmates had gone to sleep, he got down on the floor and began to ask God if He could forgive him. All of a sudden, everything inside him broke loose. He hadn't cried for years, but that night, the fountain of his heart and eyes broke loose, and he began to cry and weep and did not care who heard him. He said that night, a peace came into his heart that he had never known in all his life before and that he was now happier in prison with Jesus in his heart than he had ever been out on the street without Him.

I went about once a month over a period of two or three years and visited with these two in the visit hall. I would look around at all the other men, many of them just-as-young men, and my heart began to long after them and want to help them. I would walk up to the red brick walls of that old prison, and my eyes would almost tear up with a longing. "Oh God, I want in there!" Broken lives were in there that had never had the chance that I had enjoyed of growing up in the best Christian home in America. I thought continually of what I might have been had I been raised in their shoes.

For probably around two years, while I continued to supervise a crew of rough workman on construction sites, my heart was being drawn out of me to another group of men. I knew down deep inside that God was closing a door and opening another, but I did not know just what and where that door would be. I found out when the door finally did open that the reason it didn't open sooner was because it was not on its hinges yet. I walked into this prison as a volunteer just as the construction crews that built it were pulling away.

But let me go back to the calling of God. In the early spring of 1998, I was called to hold a ten-day revival meeting in Ohio. The seventeen-million-dollar project I had been working on was nearing completion, and I knew others would carry it on to completion. On a Friday morning, I went into the office and told the owner of the company I was leaving for two weeks for a meeting and that when I returned, if I did, I would no longer be serving as a job superintendent. When I walked across the parking lot that Friday afternoon away from that large high school addition and gigantic auditorium, I saw, as distinctly as it had been in the flesh, a huge hand go up against the auditorium wall; I knew I would never return.

The first morning of that revival after preaching the night before, I went to the basement of the house where we were staying and spilled my heart out to God. I wept, I cried, I laid all my reasons out before God. "Oh God, You know this is not comfortable to me. I know without a doubt that Your hand went up and that the door behind me is closed. I have walked away from a good salaried job with many benefits, and I see no door open before me. I have a family to take care of, and I don't know how I am to do that. But God, *I will obey You!*" With that said, indescribable billows of heavenly peace rolled through my soul, and I knew I was obeying God completely. The next morning, I went to the same prayer spot and prayed it all over again. Again the billows of heavenly peace rolled and rolled. The next morning, I did the same, and the next, and the next, for the whole ten days.

At the close of that meeting, the same Hand was pointing straight ahead. I went to the state capital to the man in charge of all the state chaplains and explained how I was feeling. He looked me over and said, "I'll tell you what to do. Sixteen miles from your house, they are building a brand-new prison—the largest in the state. Go in and volunteer, that's the way in the door." I was welcomed in, for as yet there was no Protestant chaplain at all. In the very first service with those men, I knew I was gloriously in the center of God's will.

And so, I volunteered and volunteered and still no door opened for any income. Have you ever seen a volunteer's paycheck? A year and a half later, we had sold the little farm where we raised our family and were building a new home a few miles from there. One day, as I was working on the house, an anxiety attack came over me. I felt I must have missed some further direction or provision of God. I dropped what I was doing and said to myself, "Somewhere, I have missed God's voice. I know His hand went up, I know He blessed me out of myself when I turned my all over to Him, but somewhere, I have missed a turn for no door is opening. I am going upstairs in this unfinished house and praying until I hear again from God." No stairway was in place yet, but as my foot stepped off the top rung of the ladder onto the upper floor, a huge Hand came over me.

"Son, didn't you turn this over to Me?"

"Yes, Lord, I did."

"What are you going to do with it now?"

"Lord, here, I give it back to You."

Immediately, those same billows of heavenly peace began to roll and roll through my soul. I went back down the ladder and to work again. A few days later, I found in the mailbox a small envelope from someone in another state that I did not know either then or now and cannot remember the name. Inside the envelope was a check made out to my name for $5,000. I thought, *What is the mistake here?*

And here came that big Hand again. "Didn't I tell you I would take care of you?"

Just as that was running low, the man I had talked to in the capital a year and a half before stopped into my office in the prison. "Chaplain, I want to tell you something. When I heard what God is doing with you here in the prison, my heart rejoiced. Are you ready? You are going on the payroll today!"

And that is how God has led me for the past twenty-two years into what will likely be a life sentence where I had never thought I would be. Romans 11:34: "For who hath known the mind of the Lord? Or who hath been his counselor?"

It was certainly a blessing to have had the opportunity to steer William Cawman to the chaplaincy, initially as a volunteer and then on the payroll as a state chaplain. Over the years, it has been even a greater blessing to witness how God has called Bill into the work He has set before him.

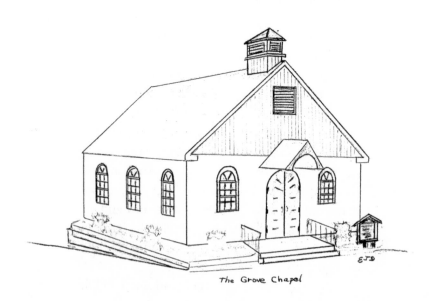

The Grove Chapel

CHAPTER 21

CALLED TO SERVE

Let brotherly love continue. Be not forgetful to entertain
strangers; for thereby some have entertained angels unawares.

—Hebrews 13:1–2

I recall many conversations I had with my mother with respect to hospitality. It was my mother's desire to have missionaries, evangelists, and guest speakers at our house for dinner. She wasn't always able to do so, but I know she wanted to. She would always say, "You never know if one of these guests are angels."

I am blessed to have a helpmate who enjoys cooking. Together, we have enjoyed having guests for dinner. I can't say that we have been able to identify any of our dinner guests as angels. However, the possibility of such an event is truly intriguing.

I do remember one dinner guest that was memorable. However, it was not memorable for being a positive experience. At one point in time, my wife and I were searching for a church. We were in a church service, and the pastor's sermon on one particular Sunday was based on a passage in the Revelation. I knew the sermon was truly a debacle. After the service, I approached an elderly friend of the family. I asked this lady what she thought of the sermon. Without hesitation, and loudly, she said, "He's all mixed up." I thought her response was spot on. However, the situation required a deeper investigation. Therefore, my wife and I invited the pastor and his wife for dinner. During dinner, I asked about some of the details of the pastor's sermon on the Revelation. The pastor admitted that it was difficult for him to preach on the Revelation because (in his words) "the book is full of fairy tales." Let me just say the remainder of our dinner was full of debate with very little dessert. As you can imagine, our search for a new church continued.

Our home church did something unique with regards to hospitality. We had a number of young couples in our church. Our young couples' group had a range of ages it was supposed to represent. However, as the older couples started to exceed the upper range, we kept moving the age up to include the same group of couples. One of the key activities of the young couples group was hospitality. Even though our church had the typical complement of ushers, the young couples group decided to expand into its own hospitality committee. Young couples would sign up as a welcoming couple. The welcoming couple would plan on having company for dinner on the Sunday of their choosing. They would attend church that Sunday and look for any new families in attendance. If there were any visitors, the young couple would invite them to their home for dinner. If there were no visitors on that Sunday, or if there were visitors and they declined the invitation for dinner, the host couple would look around and invite someone for dinner. This hospitality endeavor was a tremendous success. The process was not a burden. The dinner invitation ended up being scheduled for a couple about once every three months. It was fun knowing that you were planning to have someone for dinner, maybe someone new looking for a church or someone you knew or someone you just wanted to get to know better.

The young couples' plan for hospitality was a key factor in growth for that church. Do you recall the number of times you visited a church and, as part of the welcoming to that church, you were invited to someone's home for dinner? Maybe never. However, do you recall the number of times you visited a church and no one went out of the way to say hello?

—⟨∞⟩—

In this section of "Called to Serve," I have found it interesting how God has brought friends and coworkers into similar ministries. Rev. Jonathan and Gail Haslett are a couple of like-minded Christians who responded to God's calling in ministry that seemed to crisscross with our ministries. Gail Haslett was a teacher to our children in Massachusetts, and later in her career, she taught our grandchildren in New Jersey. Jonathan was a pastor who came to the end of a particular pastorate and ended up now serving as the supervising chaplain at the state prison where I started in my prison ministry. The following is a portion of how Gail Haslett describes their journey:

> The path I have traveled has been rewarding, though at times bumpy and painful. Through all I have experienced, I have held on to the words from Proverbs 3:5–6, "Trust in the Lord with all your heart and lean not on your own understanding; in all your ways acknowledge him, and he shall direct your path." God has used other Christians to guide and encourage me to accept challenges I would never attempt on my own.
>
> My journey began when I was in high school. My family had attended several different churches while I was growing up. I remember

memorizing the twenty-third and hundredth Psalm and singing songs like "Onward Christian Soldiers;" however, I never remember hearing about the forgiveness of sin or a personal relationship with Christ. That all changed when my sister's boyfriend's mother shared the Gospel with my mother. After that, my family started attending a church that had Sunday and Wednesday evening services. We rarely missed a service. My mother accepted Christ, and there was a visible change in her that others noticed. The change was so dramatic that I wanted to experience that same change in my life. I accepted Christ during a one-on-one Bible study with a missionary home on furlough.

Before I came to know the Lord, I had not given much thought to what I was going to do after high school. I was an ego-centered teenager. Learning had not been easy for me, especially reading. When I was in elementary school, my parents were told I would never be more than a C student, so college was not even on my radar. Then I believe the Lord gave me the confidence to apply to college. I wanted to go to a Christian college because I wanted to grow as a Christian and develop friendships with those who shared my beliefs. I chose to apply to only one college, Gordon College. I chose that college because my pastor and his wife graduated from there. There was one problem; my guidance counselor told me I would not get into Gordon College, and if I did, I would never last. God proved him wrong! I graduated in the top third of my class with a BS in elementary education. The highlight of my time at Gordon came during my sophomore year when my resident assistant approached me about becoming a resident assistant for the following year. I saw myself as quiet and insecure. I was surprised to learn that someone saw me as a potential leader. I went ahead and applied and was chosen. I flourished in my new role, and God used me to minister to the girls on my floor, especially the freshmen.

After graduation, I taught in a Christian school in Lynn, Massachusetts, for five years. I taught a combined class of first-and second-graders. It was challenging to meet the needs of students of two different grades, especially since there were varying abilities within each grade level. To make it more challenging, one year, I had a student from Nigeria (his father attended the seminary) who did not speak much English. God gave me patience and creative ideas to make learning fun and accessible to my students. While I was at the school, I was asked to supervise a student teacher and to present a workshop on Making Manipulative Bulletin Boards at the teacher's convention. These were new experiences for me and totally out of my comfort zone, but God gave me the confidence and ability to do them both. During my third year, I started to get restless and decided that perhaps I should pursue a master's degree in religious education from Gordon Conwell. I was twenty-nine, and in the back of my mind, I remember a former pastor telling me if you want to get married, go where the guys are. That fall, I stepped out in faith and took New Testament Survey. When I got to class, I found that I was too shy and too embarrassed to talk to any of the guys. But it turned out to be good advice, because there was a guy in the class that also attended the same singles Bible study I did. We started talking at the Bible study, later started sitting together in class, and then we dated. We were married that August. That guy's name was Jonathan Haslett. I never did get an MRE (Masters' of Religious Education), but I did get an MRS.

Later in time, we left West Virginia and headed for a new church ministry in New Jersey. We went to the new church broken and not sure what the future would hold, but we jumped right in and did the best we could. There was a solid group of pastors in the area that Jon got involved with, and I took a part-time job doing only the teaching at a daycare/preschool. I enjoyed the teaching part of the job, but I missed the Christian atmosphere. I decided not to renew my contract. Around that time, my first-grade daughter was diagnosed with a learning disability and was placed in a special learning lab. Over the summer, I started working with her intensely using the rhythmic writing and all other materials I had accumulated over the years. In the fall, she continued attending the public school, and I continued working with her at home. By the end of the school year, she had exceeded their expectations, and they planned to return her to the regular classroom.

With my daughter caught up academically, I started to feel the desire to teach once again. I visited two Christian schools in the area. Then one day, I was talking on the phone to my former principal in Massachusetts. She mentioned that Jim DuBois (who had been a parent of one of my students in Massachusetts) had gone to a Christian school not far from where we lived. We had never been to that town and knew nothing about that Christian school. We looked up the information and found it was only a half an hour away, which was doable. I was hired to be one of their second-grade teachers. When my daughter was tested for admission, I was a bit nervous that her scores would not meet the standards of the school. She did fine, and the tester even remarked on what a good reader she was. God allowed me to use my gift of teaching to help my daughter to succeed. Now I was facing the challenge of balancing home, school, and church. God gave me the ability to do it all, though there were many late nights.

Later in time, while Jon was working part-time in a church, Jim DuBois contacted him about a part-time chaplain position. Jon was offered the job and took it. Now Jon had two part-time jobs in the ministry he thought he had left. Both jobs were a half an hour from our house, but in different directions. Things at the church were going well, and attendance started to increase. Though I helped where I could, I was not as involved as I had been in the past, and since Jon was doing two jobs, he was limited on how much he could do. For the first time in church ministry, we felt loved and accepted, not for what we did but for who we were. It was very healing.

Being a prison chaplain was challenging yet rewarding for Jon. He enjoyed writing sermons, preparing Bible studies, counseling, and being able to play his guitar while singing with the inmates. When his supervisor was leaving the prison, she encouraged him to apply for the job, which he did. It appeared that God was directing

Jon to take the chaplain supervisor position and leave the church ministry once again.

Over the years, Jim DuBois contacted Jon and invited him to preach at the church he pastored. If Jon did not have any other commitments, he would fill in, and I would go as well. One time, when we went to his church, we saw two couples we had known previously. Both couples had been members at the church we attended a few years before. One of the women invited me to a crafter's group that met at Jim's church. I went the next week with my sewing machine, not knowing what I would find. While I was there, I saw people working on all different crafts, but mostly sewing projects. All the projects that were made would eventually be given away. One woman had just learned how to make a pillowcase-style dress and showed me how to make one as well. I enjoyed being creative and made about ten of them. Then another woman became my quilt mentor. She taught me different quilt patterns as well as specific techniques. After that, a man showed me how to knit a hat on a circular loom. Transportation became a problem, so I stopped attending. I continued the various crafts I learned, but less frequently. I enjoyed teaching Sunday school and preparing for VBS but felt like something was missing. One day, my daughter told me about an after-school program that a woman in her church helped with. I contacted the director and learned that she had been praying for someone to work with the children preschool through first grade. These children had quite different lives from the children I had taught in Christian schools. It took me a while to adjust. I constantly tried new things to improve their attention while I told Bible stories or tried to do special activities. There can still be challenging days, but overall, the children are more receptive. Volunteering has opened other new and rewarding opportunities where I can use my abilities and make a difference. For now, I feel I am doing what God has called me to do, and I can honestly say God works all things together for good (Romans 8:28)!

CHAPTER 22

CALLED TO BUILD

I would imagine that many pastors or church leaders would look at this chapter and say these examples are small or insignificant when compared to the massive building projects they were blessed to oversee. Probably. However, I am not seeking to focus only on the project. Rather, I trying to reflect on the way God called on church members to commit to the build.

When I was led to serve as the pastor to a small country church, there were a few deep-seated problems within the leadership. Without identifying specific people, I will set the stage by saying the women in the church were the self-appointed leaders. The men in the church were absent without leave (AWOL). My wife and I always laughed at the fact that the church had pink plates, cups, and saucers in the kitchen. This little fact seemed to emulate the attitude that the church was considered to be okay for the women and children. Hence, the men were comfortable in sending their children to Sunday school and church while they were AWOL.

Over a period of time, God began working on some of the men in the church. During a particular summer vacation Bible school, the large number of children in attendance set in motion a movement among the men to expand the church by adding some desperately needed classrooms. The very idea of a building project was a massive undertaking for such a small church. There was a time when arguments among the women would put a stop to the painting of a room just because of the disputed color of the paint. Now, the church was getting behind a complete building project.

During a January annual business meeting, this small church voted in favor of a building project that would more than double the size of the original church structure. The concept was submitted to an architect. The architectural firm donated the costs associated with the design. The men of the church took on the challenge to build a full basement and upper level complex with ten classrooms, one mechanical room, two bathrooms, and two offices. The men and women worked every Saturday starting in June, with the final dedication of the project on Thanksgiving of the same year. Only one subcontractor was hired to hang the sheetrock. Otherwise, the men and women in the church constructed the entire building project. Would it be a coincidence that the church had within its membership a mason, a union plumber, a union electrician, and a former homebuilder? Or was this a God-incidence? I still recall the words of the mason at the conclusion of the building project. He said, "In all my years of construction, I have never seen a building project go so smoothly." The men in the church took pride in their work and began attending as families and began taking on appropriate leadership roles.

In our third church, we started by meeting in our living room. Over time, we began renting various facilities and ultimately grew to a point where we needed a building. The search for an appropriate facility ended with the possibility of purchasing a former rescue squad building. In order to appreciate how God led in this purchase, it is necessary that I get into the numbers. Work with me on the numbers for a couple of paragraphs to better appreciate how God was leading in this purchase.

A local real-estate agent was advertising the rescue squad building for a sale price of $300,000. We felt God was leading us to purchase this building, but we did not believe it was worth that amount of money. We offered $220,000, and they countered with $240,000. We agreed with the amount and signed the contract. We then started spending money on the land survey, building appraisal, initial stages of securing a mortgage, and ordering some furniture.

At one point, the process of purchasing the rescue squad building seemed to be falling apart. The building appraisal came in at only $200,000. Wow, that was $40,000 below the contracted agreement. The bank was not interested in providing a mortgage for any amount over the appraisal.

It was beginning to look like we would need to offset the difference between the contract agreed price and the appraisal. That's $40,000 on us. I then received a phone call from the real-estate agent. The seller needed to cancel the contract for the purchase of the building. It was discovered that the local municipality and not the rescue squad owned the building. Therefore, the municipality could only sell the building through a sealed bid process.

Given the fact that the lawyers for the municipality cancelled the contract, we were no longer obligated to the purchase price of $240,000. We then followed the appropriate procedures and entered into the sealed bid process for the purchase of the building owned by the municipality. Our sealed bid offered the appraised price for the building of $200,000. We were successful as the highest bidder given the fact that we were the one and only bidder.

The circumstances associated with the purchase of the rescue squad building at the appraised value were a complete set of coincidences. No. This was another example of God's sovereignty over circumstances for good.

And we know that all things work together for good to them that love God, to them who are the called according to His purpose. (Romans 8:28)

CHAPTER 23

CALLED TO BE FAITHFUL

It is because of the LORD's mercies that we are not
consumed, because his compassions fail not. They are
new every morning; great is thy faithfulness.

—Lamentations 3:22–23

The standard of faithfulness is an all-inspiring theme and masterfully woven into some of the greatest hymns, sermons, and books throughout Christendom. My alma mater maintains the hymn "Great is Thy Faithfulness" as its school song. I recall, as a student, some of the chapel services that had great speakers and fantastic musical artists. However, many of the greatest and uplifting times of worship included the singing of the school song.

As a matter of local history for me, Mr. Thomas O. Chisholm, the author of "Great is Thy Faithfulness," resided in my hometown. While I did not know Mr. Chisholm, a couple of members of our church did know him personally.

The biblical accounts of God's faithfulness are numerous. We know without a doubt His Word is faithful and true (Revelations 22:6). I love how God's faithfulness in Lamentations 3:22–23 is written within the context of His mercies and compassions as never failing.

As we come to conclusion of this little book, I wish to explore the measure of faithfulness to our calling. A full measure of faithfulness in our calling is without question. Refer to the following:

Faithful is he that calleth you, who also will do it.
(1 Thessalonians 5:24)

In God's sovereignty, He not only calls, and without doubt, He will do it. His plans and calling are dependent upon His determinate counsel and foreknowledge.

I love how the apostle Paul describes himself as a "prisoner of Jesus Christ" who was "made a minister, according to the gift of the grace of God given unto me by the effectual working of his power" (Ephesians 3:7).

There is a popular song entitled "Find us Faithful" where the refrain includes the phrase, "Oh, may all who come behind us find us faithful."

It is without doubt that God is faithful. In this book, I have tried to explore how God called others and me into preordained ministries. I have tried to identify pastors, missionaries, teachers, administrators, volunteers, prisoners, correctional staff, builders, musicians and, yes, even a group of crafters. Remember how Gale

Haslett described her mentors in various craft projects? Buzz Stell was Gale Haslett's instructor. Can you imagine knitting little round caps which were made and donated to a maternity ward for newborn and premature babies? This makes the biblical admonition for doing unto the least of these as doing it unto the Lord as something "small" but tangible. If the Lord should tarry, I wonder how many of those newborn and premature babies will grow up to believe in the Lord Jesus Christ as their Savior and be called by God to ministry? I was a preemie. My mother had severe physical complications with my birth. Yet she was a prayer warrior who insisted that I be named Elijah. We know the Elijah of the Bible was faithful, and it's not hard see how God's faithfulness is sufficient motivation for us to faithfully serve Him.

May it be our prayer that God will find us faithful in fulfilling His calling to work.

Wherefore, holy brethren, partakers of the heavenly calling, consider the Apostle and High Priest of our profession, Christ Jesus, Who was faithful to him that appointed him, as also Moses was faithful in all his house. (Hebrews 3:1–2)

REFERENCES

Biblical references in this book come from *The New Scofield Reference Bible*, authorized King James Version, copyright 1967, by Oxford University Press, Inc.

BOOKS AUTHORED BY
E. JAMES DUBOIS

The Pathfinder, Christian Faith Publishing, Inc., copyright 2017
The Sanctuary Cabin, Christian Faith Publishing, Inc., copyright 2020

ABOUT THE AUTHOR

 E. James DuBois is a graduate of Philadelphia Biblical University (now Cairn University) and the California Graduate School of Theology. He has served as a pastor, teacher, school administrator, state prison chaplain, coordinator of chaplaincy services, and retired from the New Jersey Department of Corrections as an assistant divisional director. Jim DuBois is a decorated Vietnam War veteran. He served as the director for the New Jersey Department of Corrections Critical Incident Stress Management Team and led this team in direct support to the New York-New Jersey Port Authority in New York City at ground zero following the attack on our country on September 11, 2001. Jim and his wife Christina have been married for fifty-three years. Their two sons are married. They have been blessed with seven grandchildren. They now reside in Kissimmee, Florida.